This Book Belongs To:

Colour Test

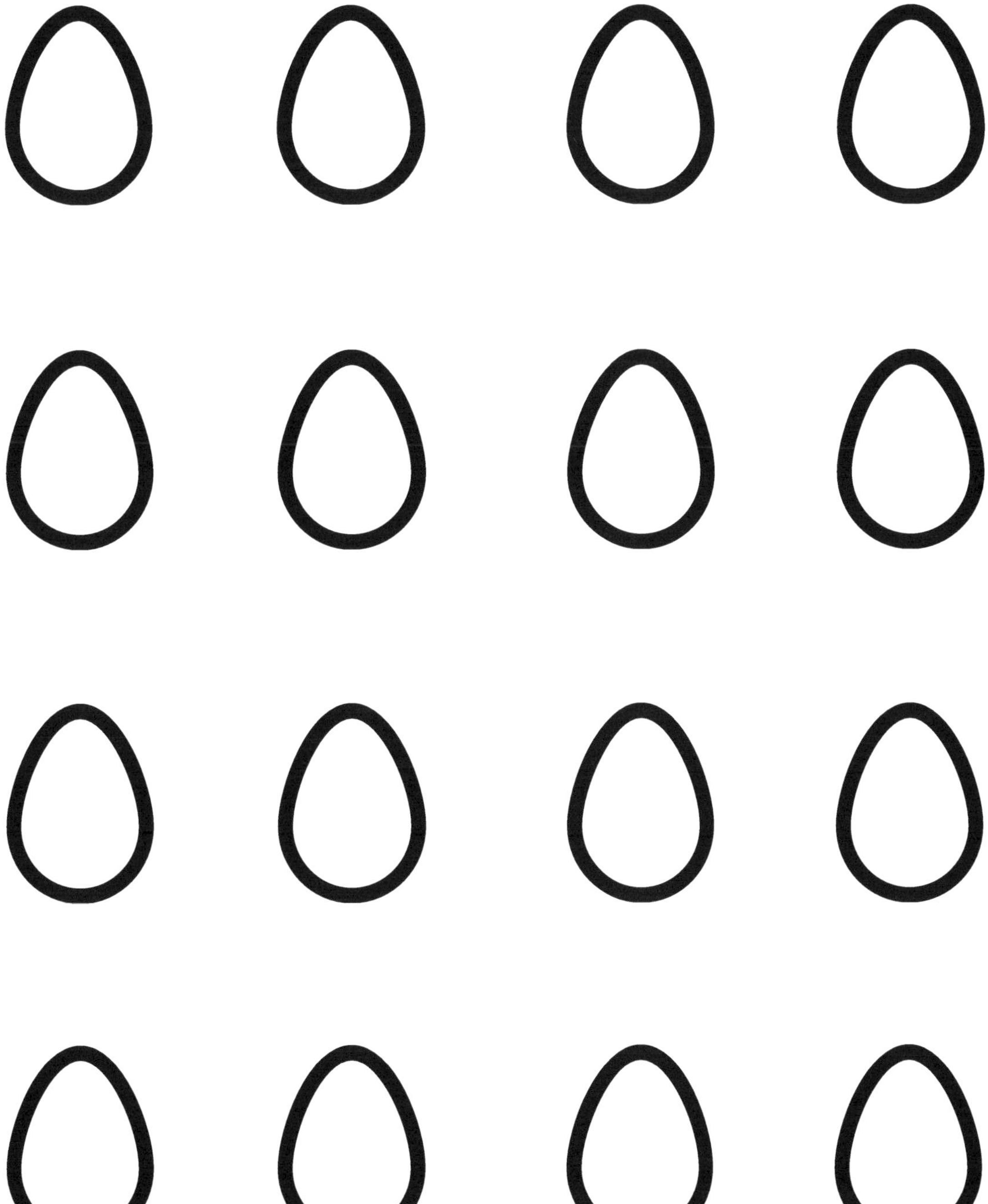

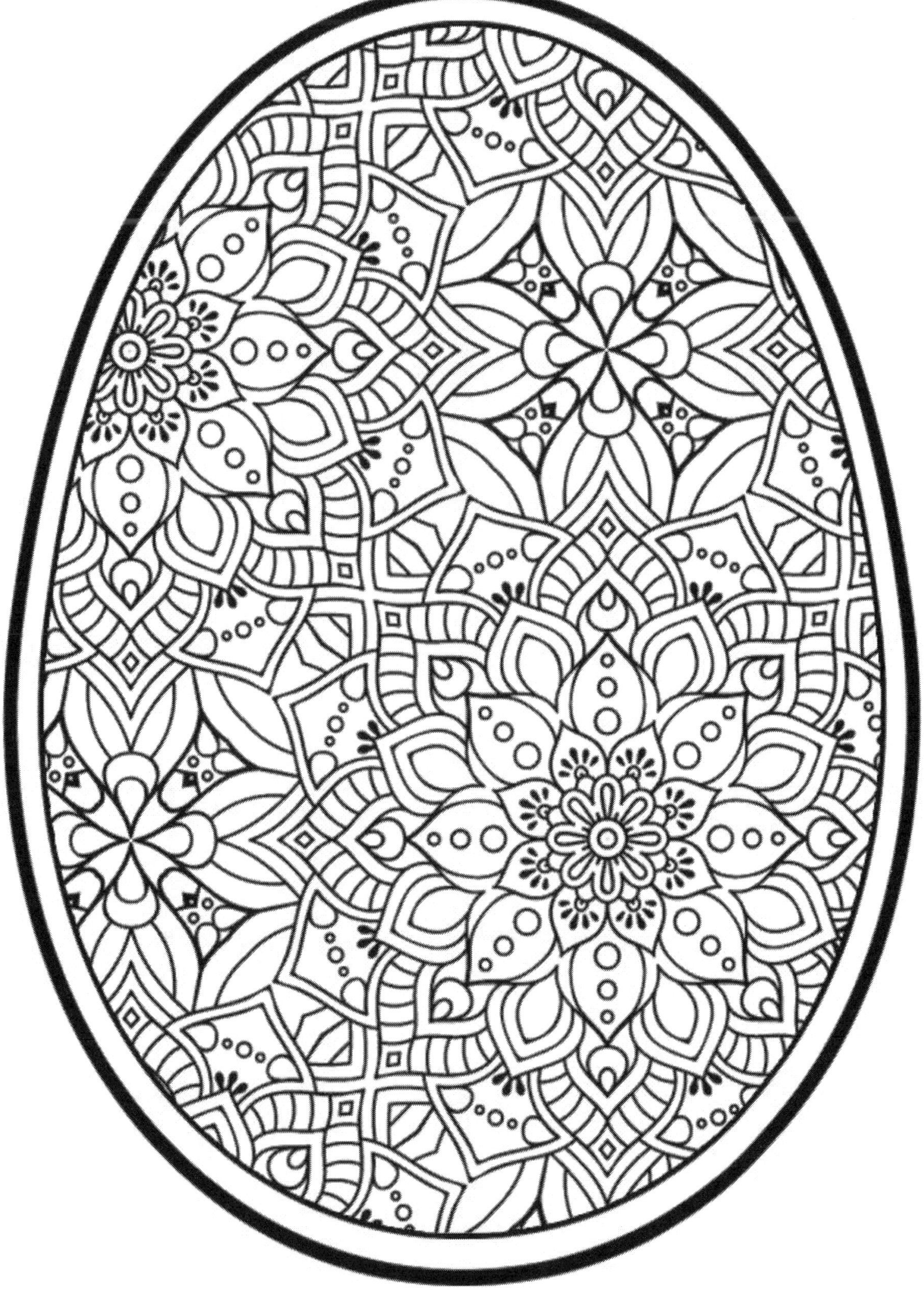

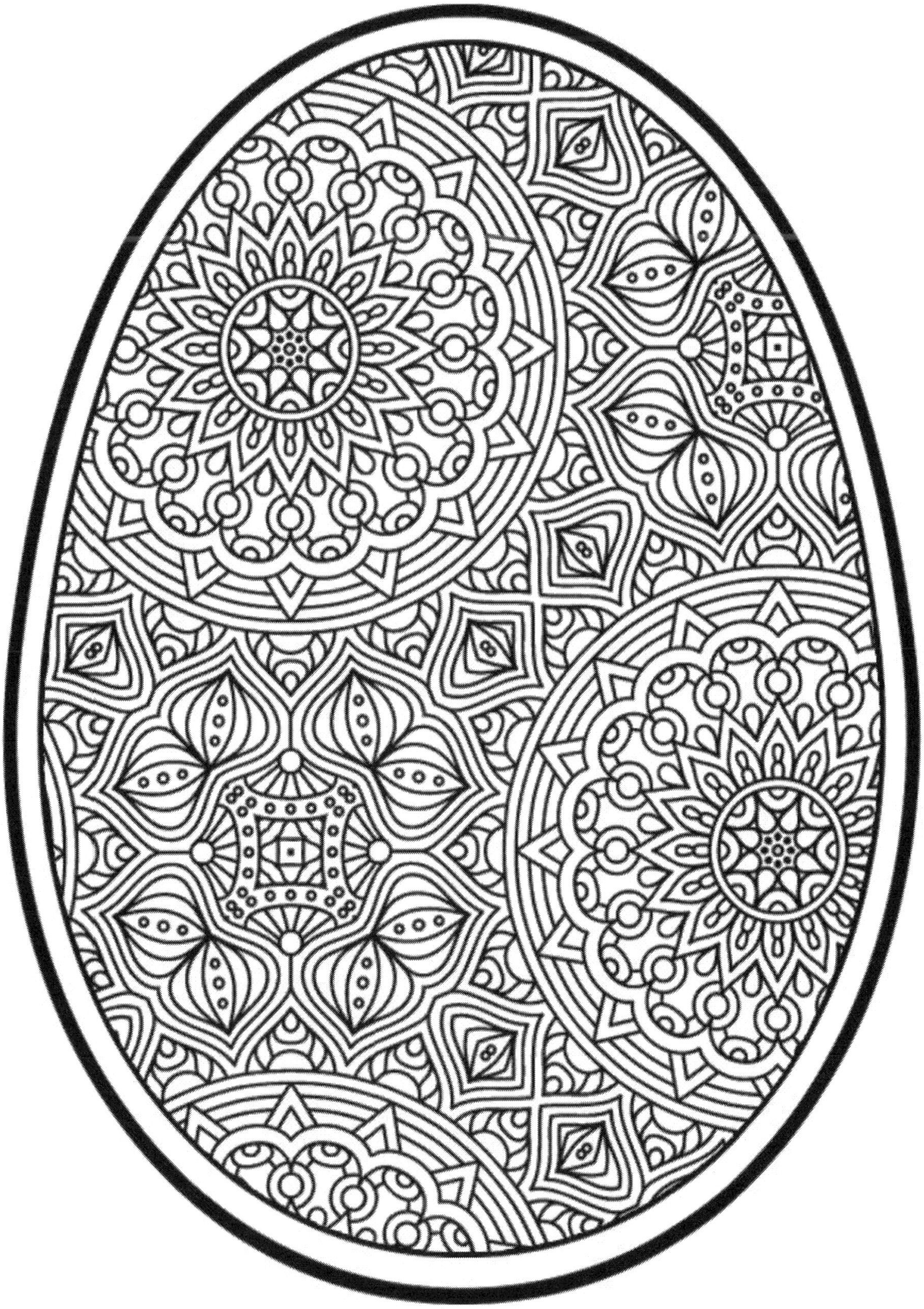

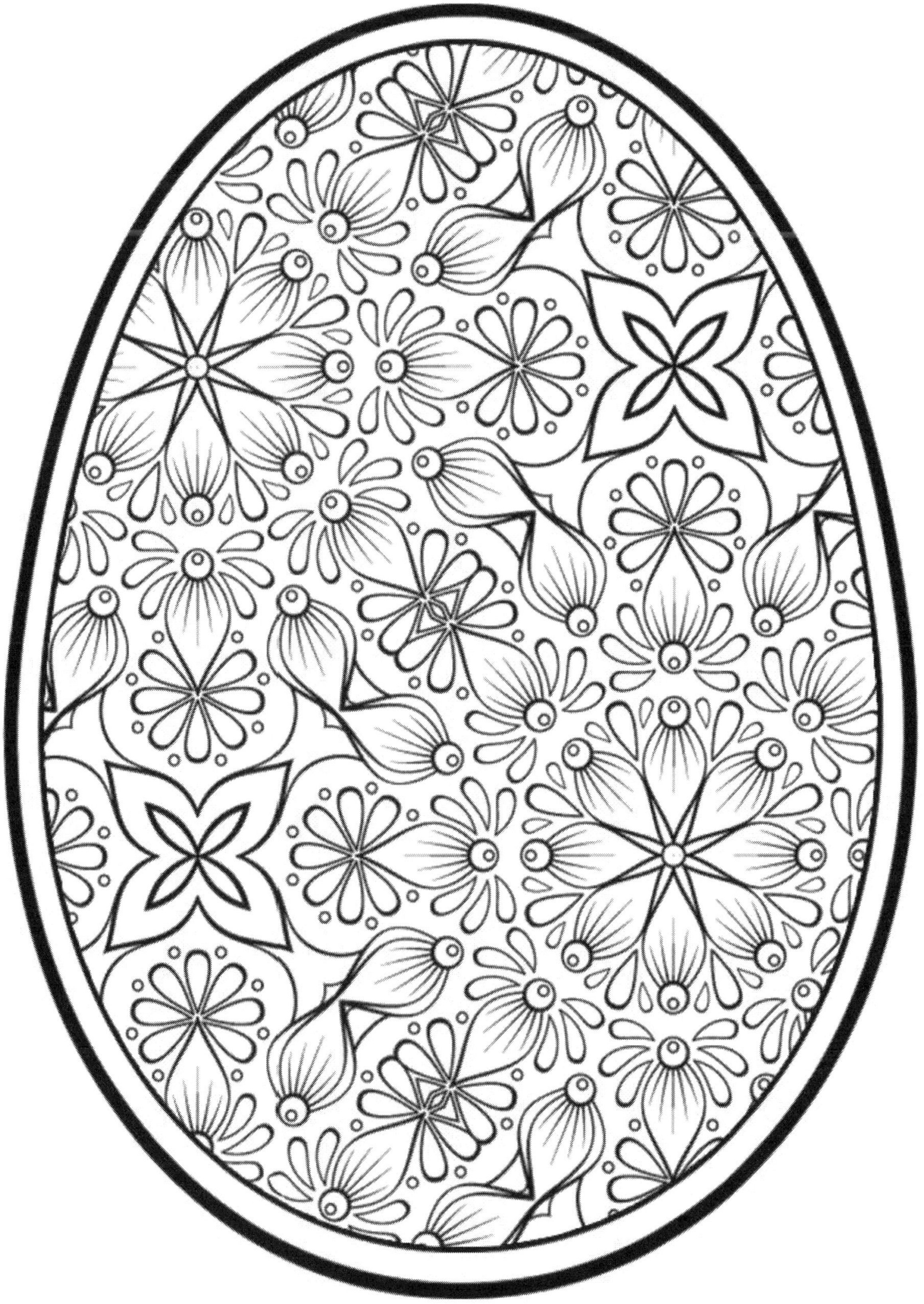

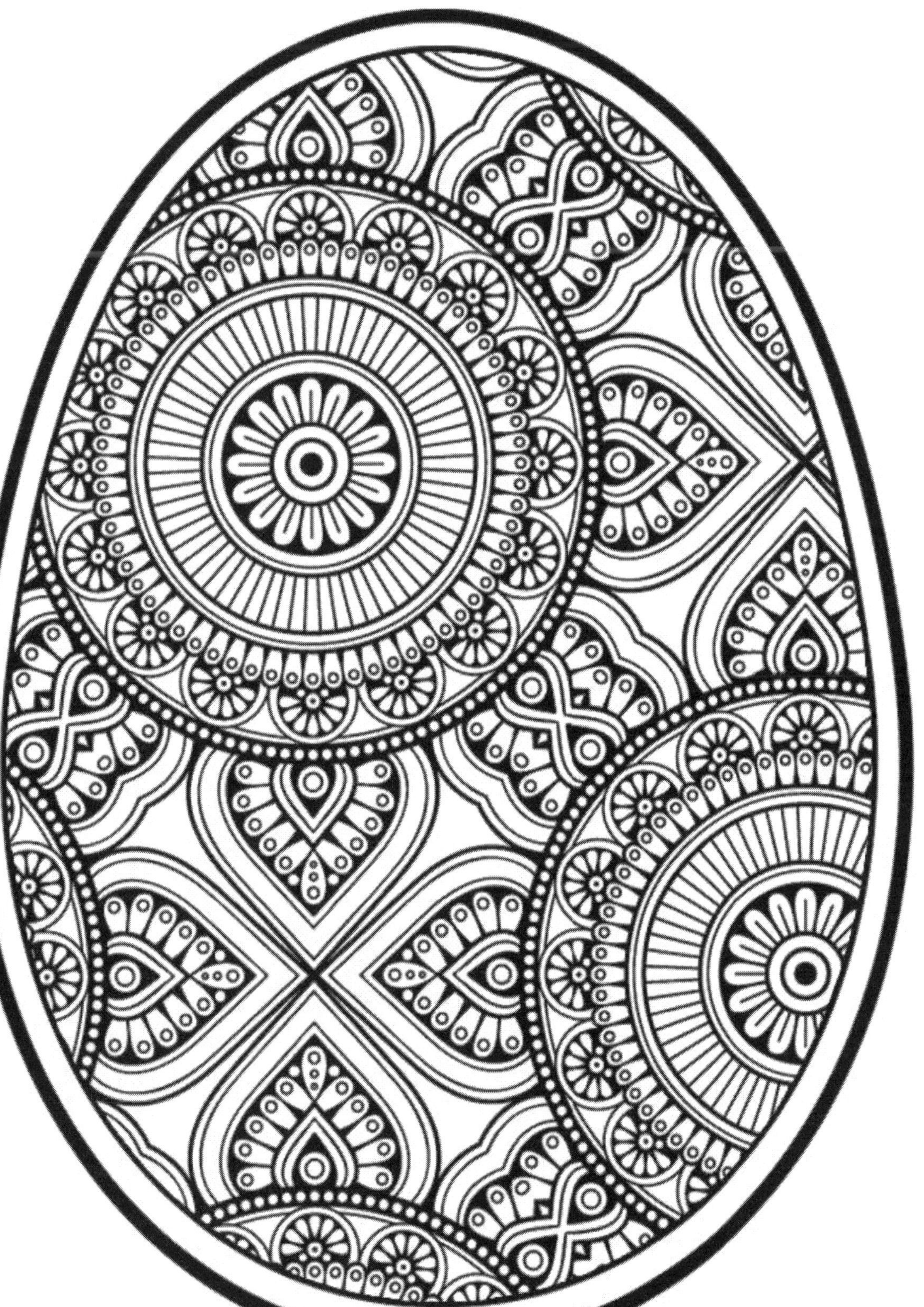

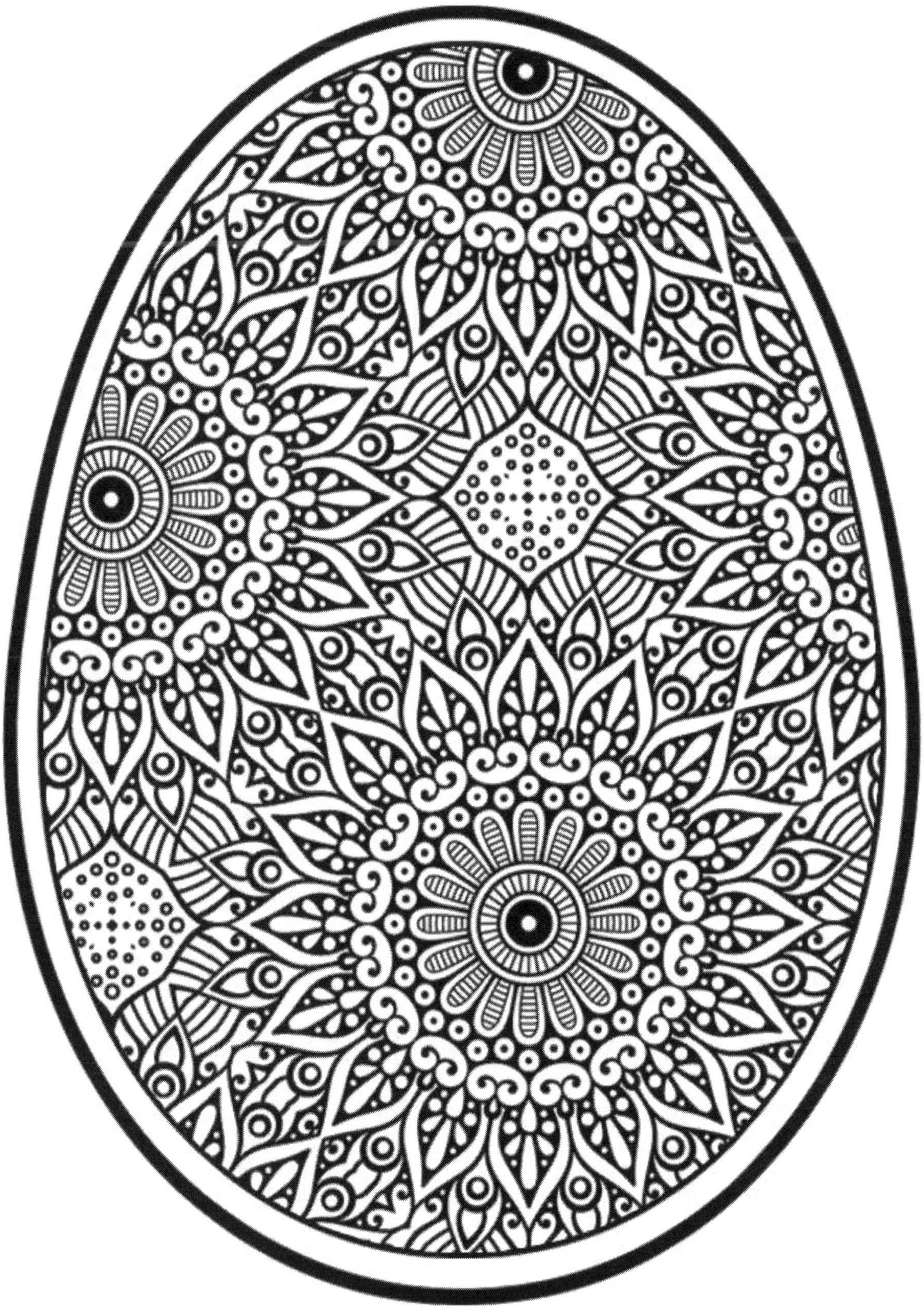

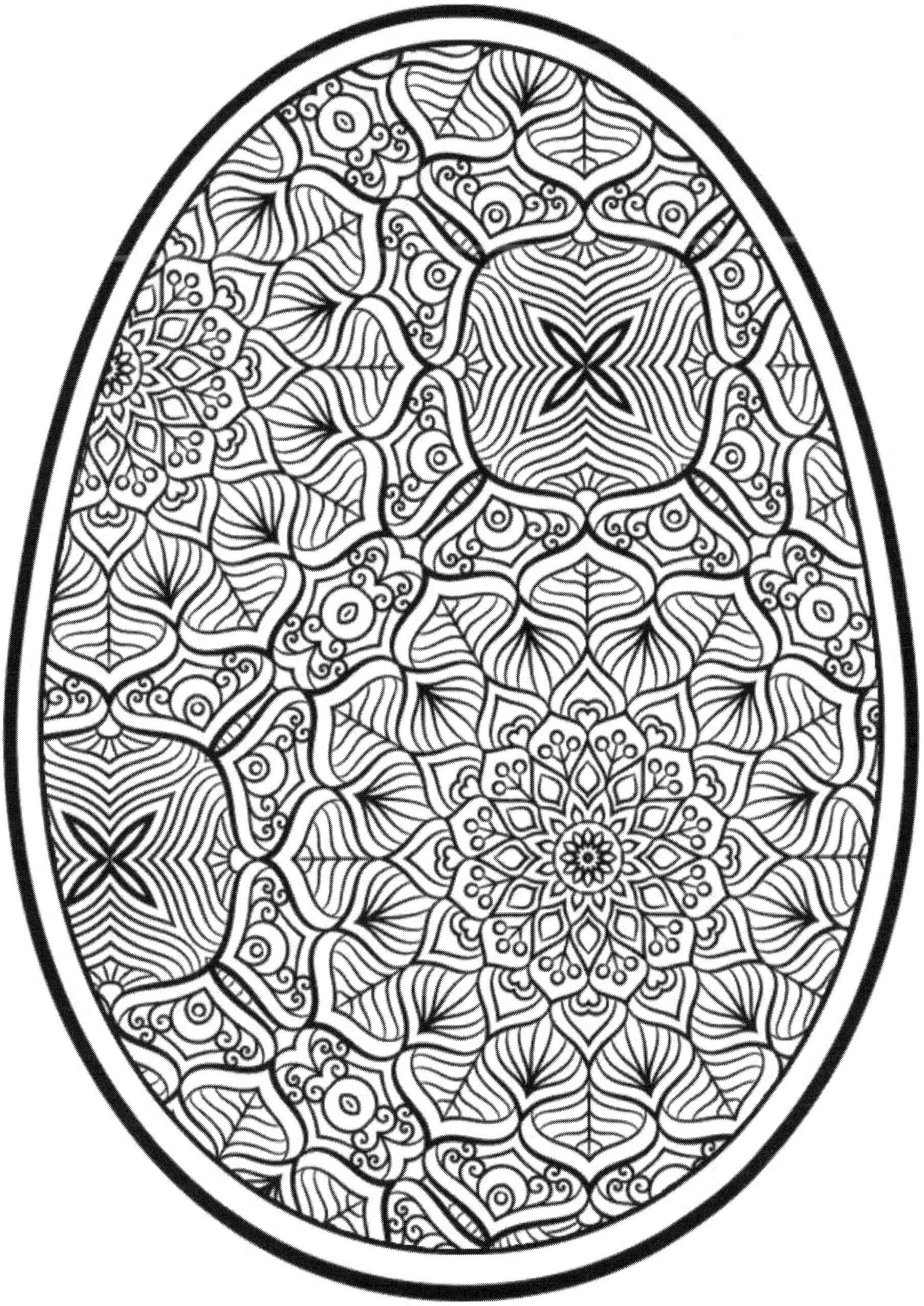

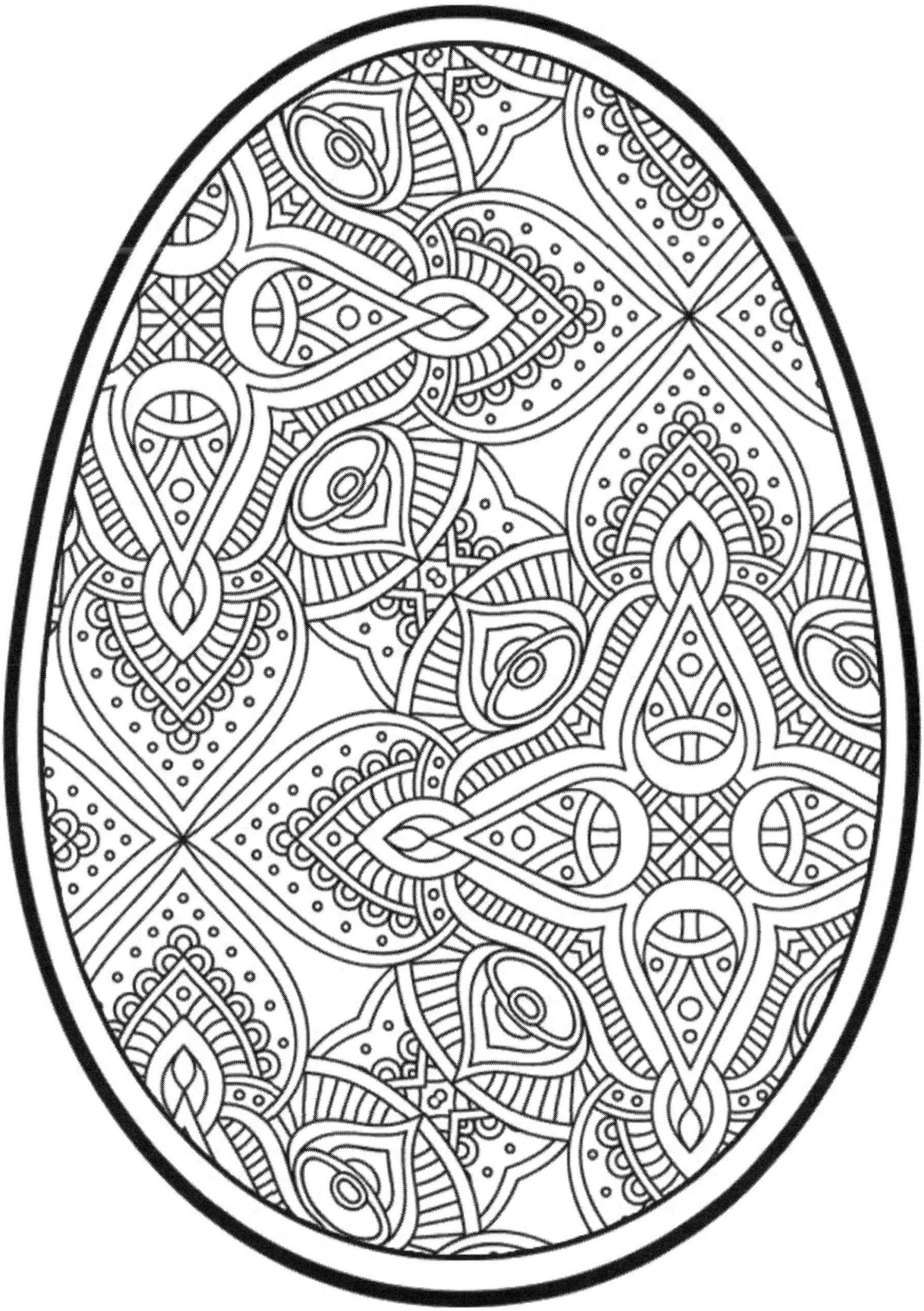

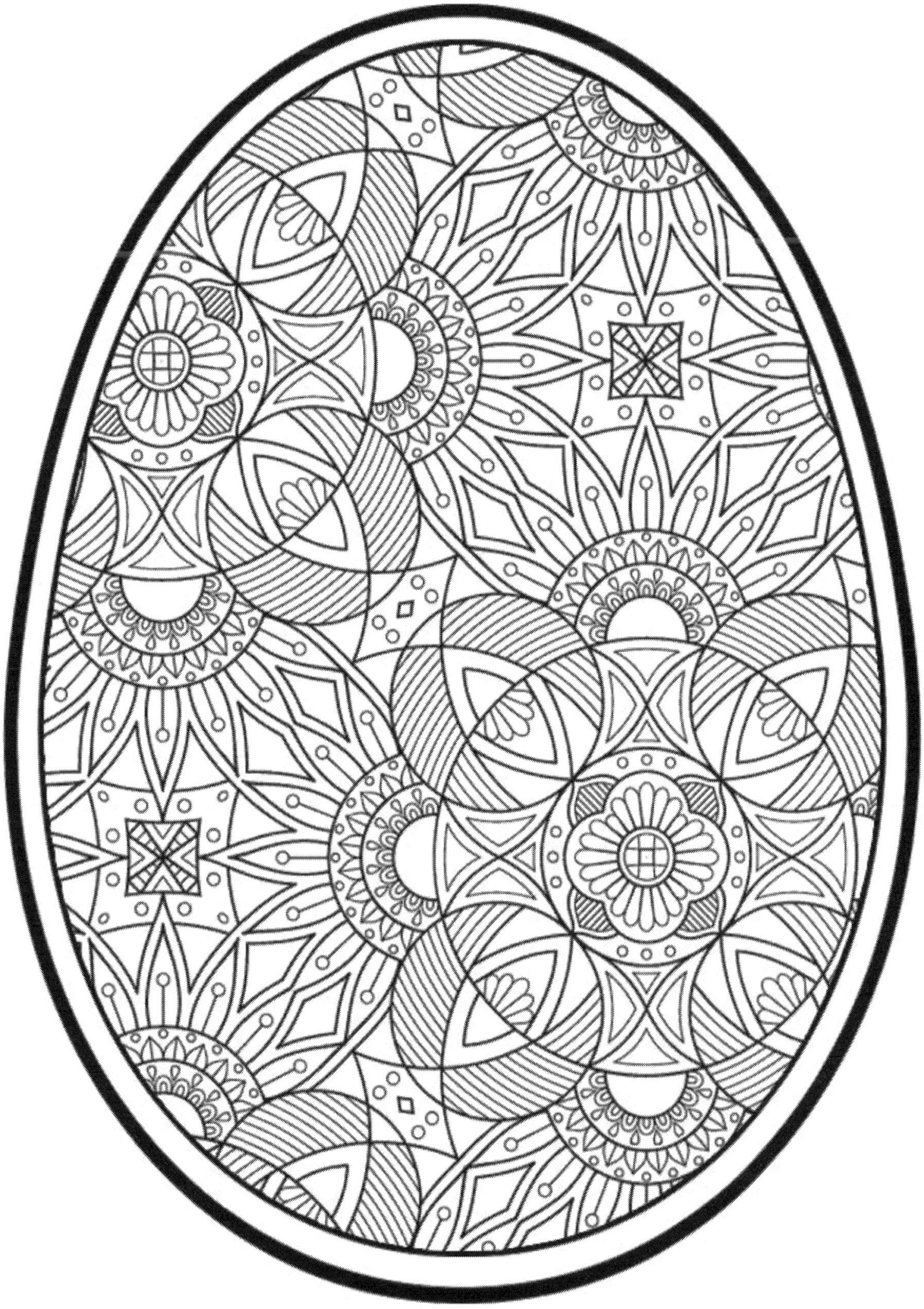

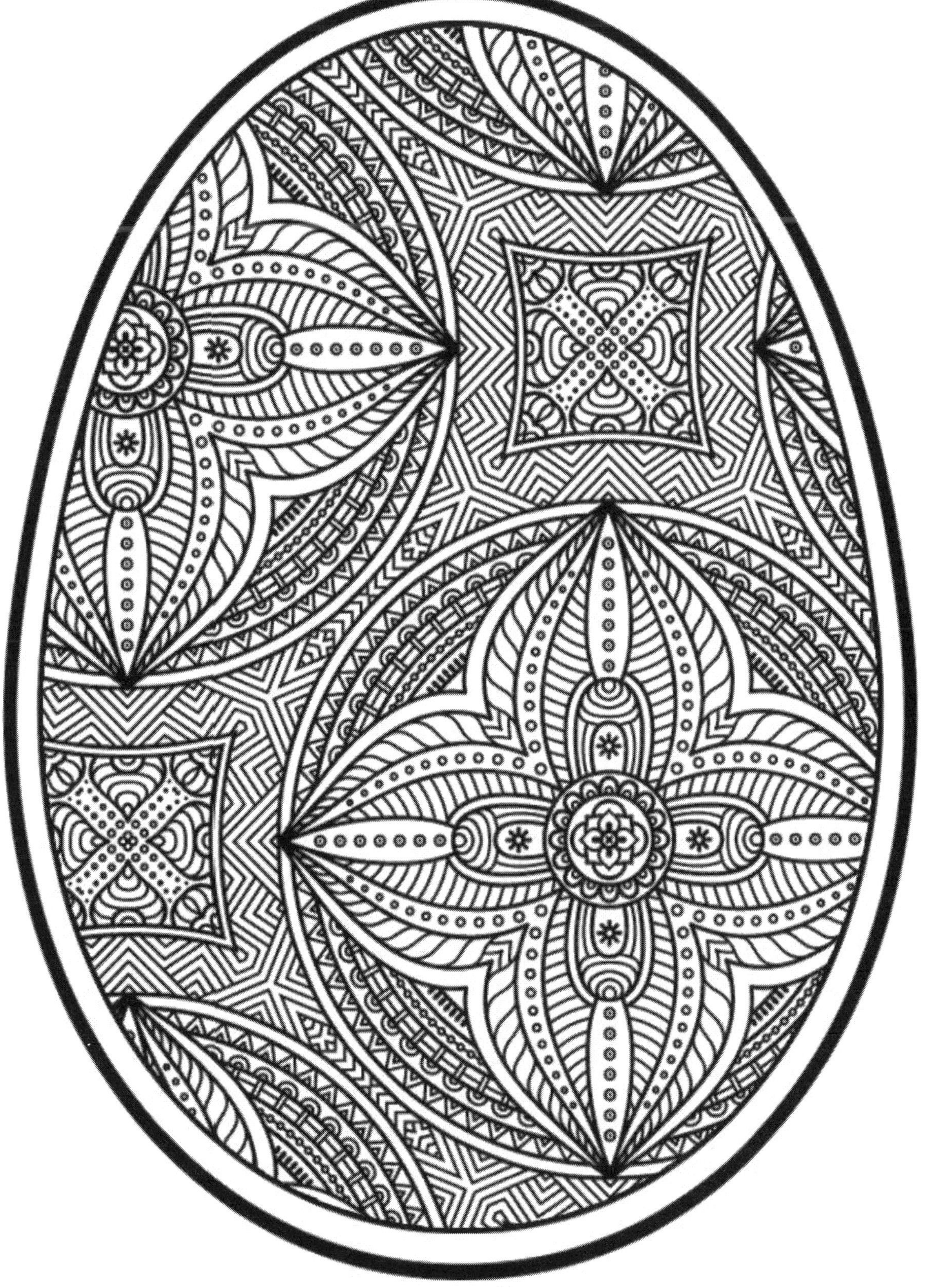

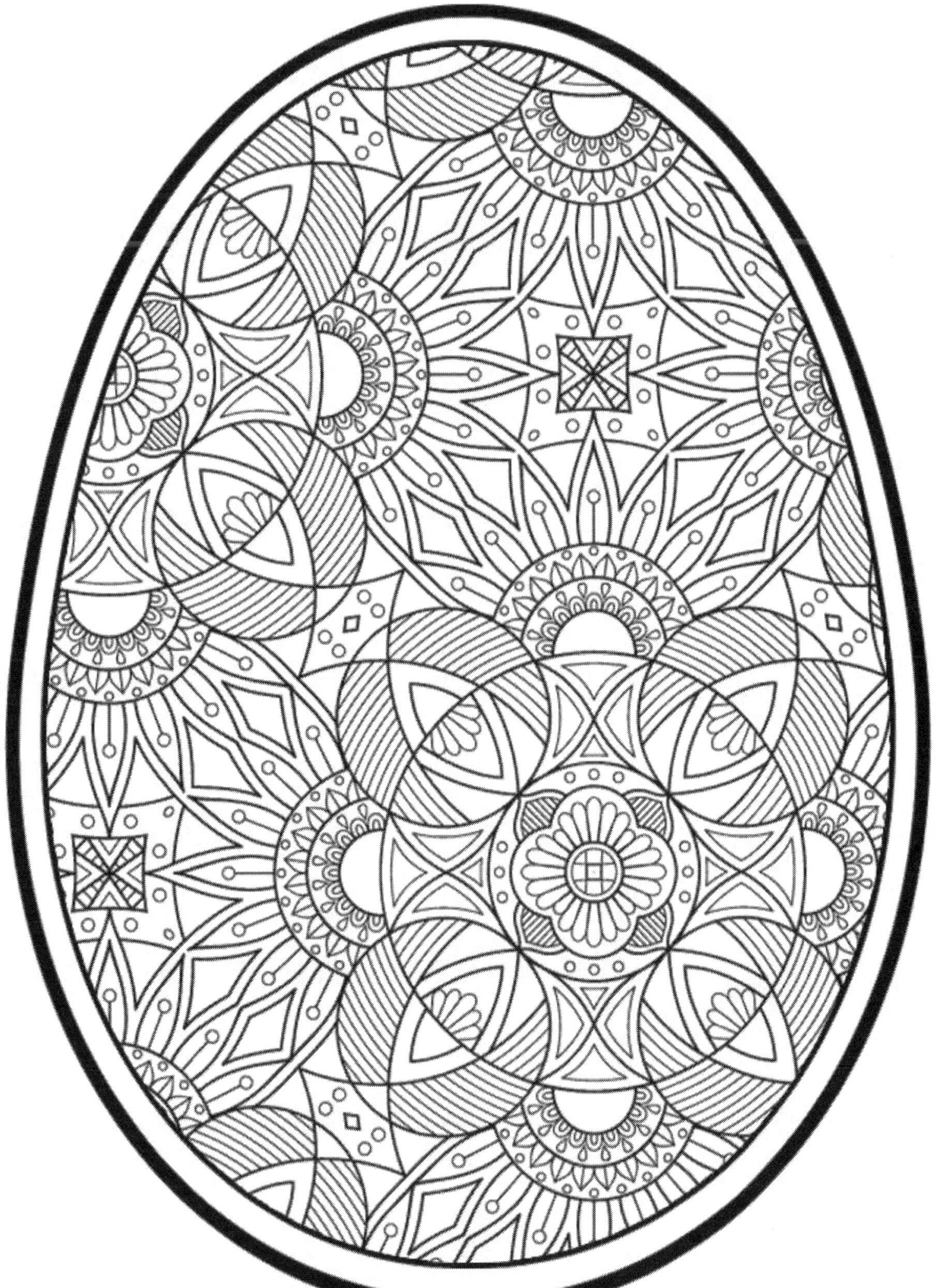

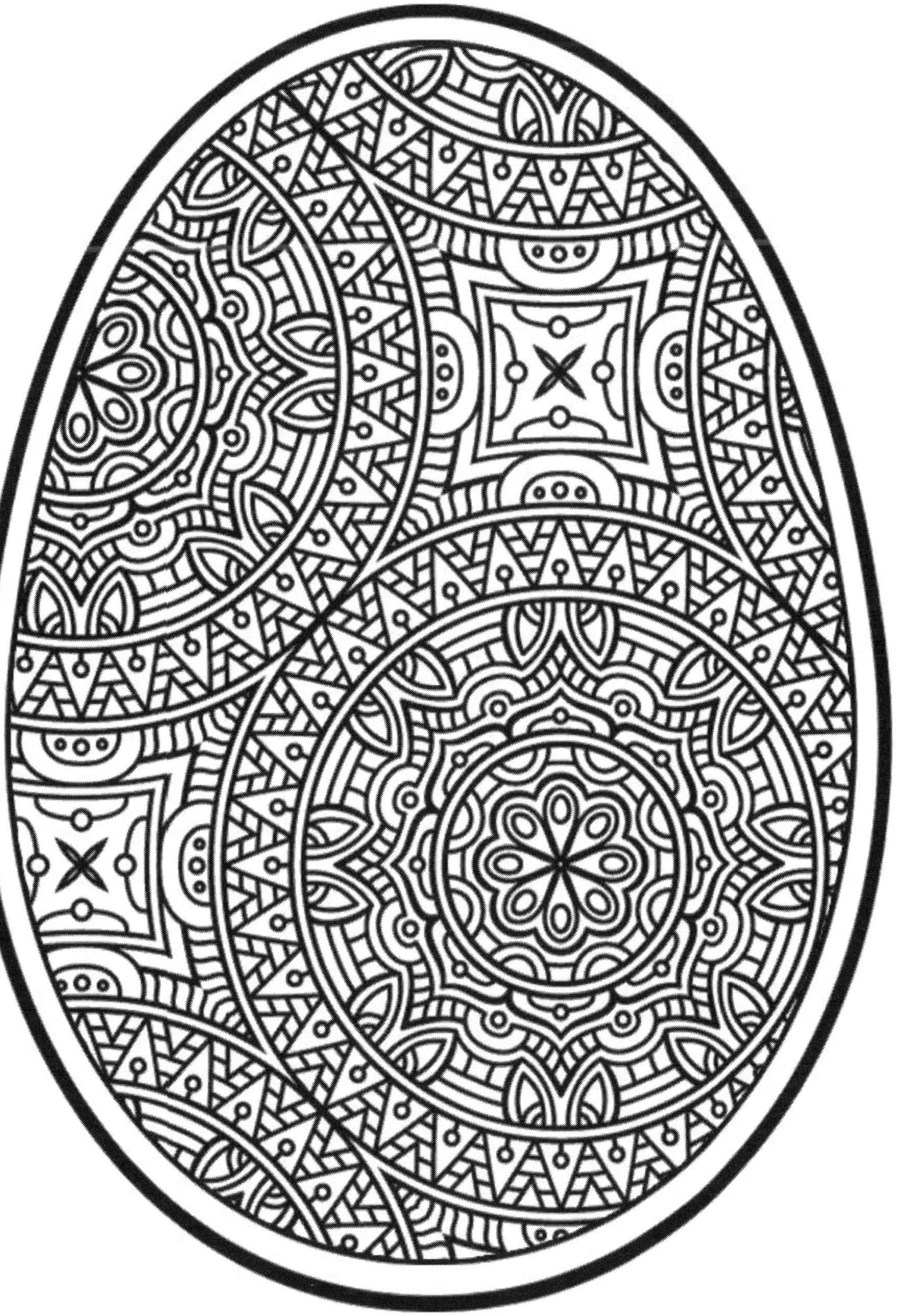

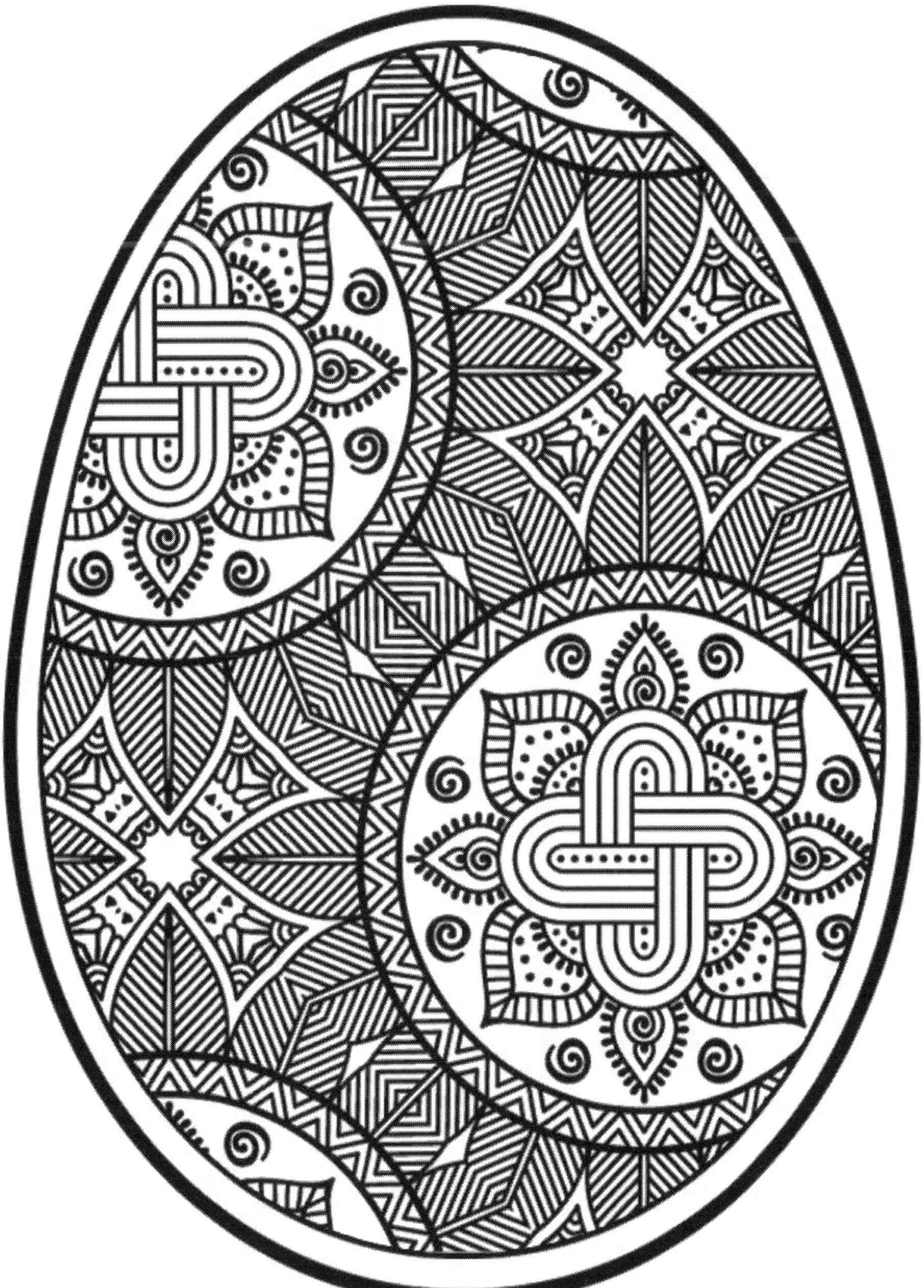

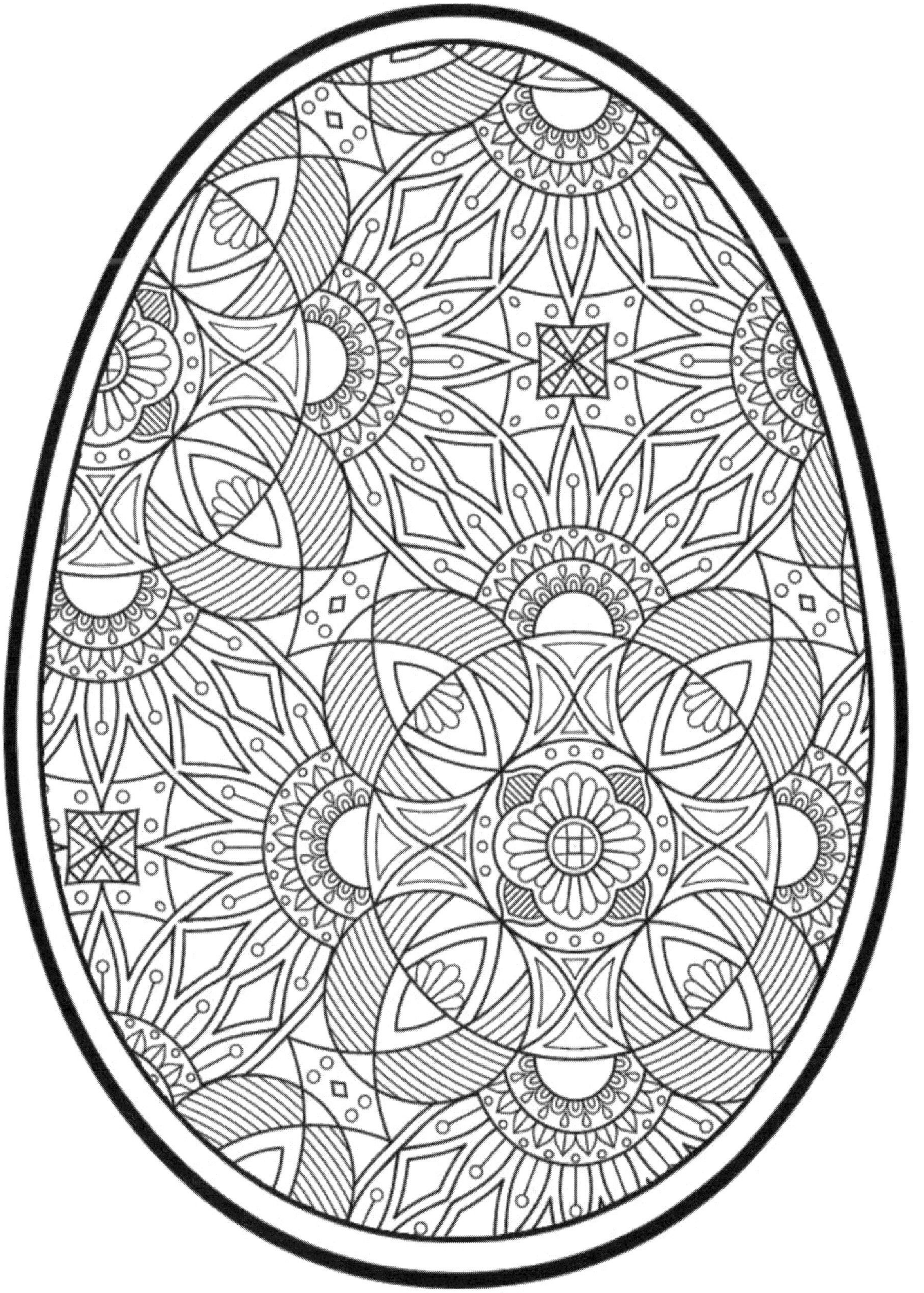

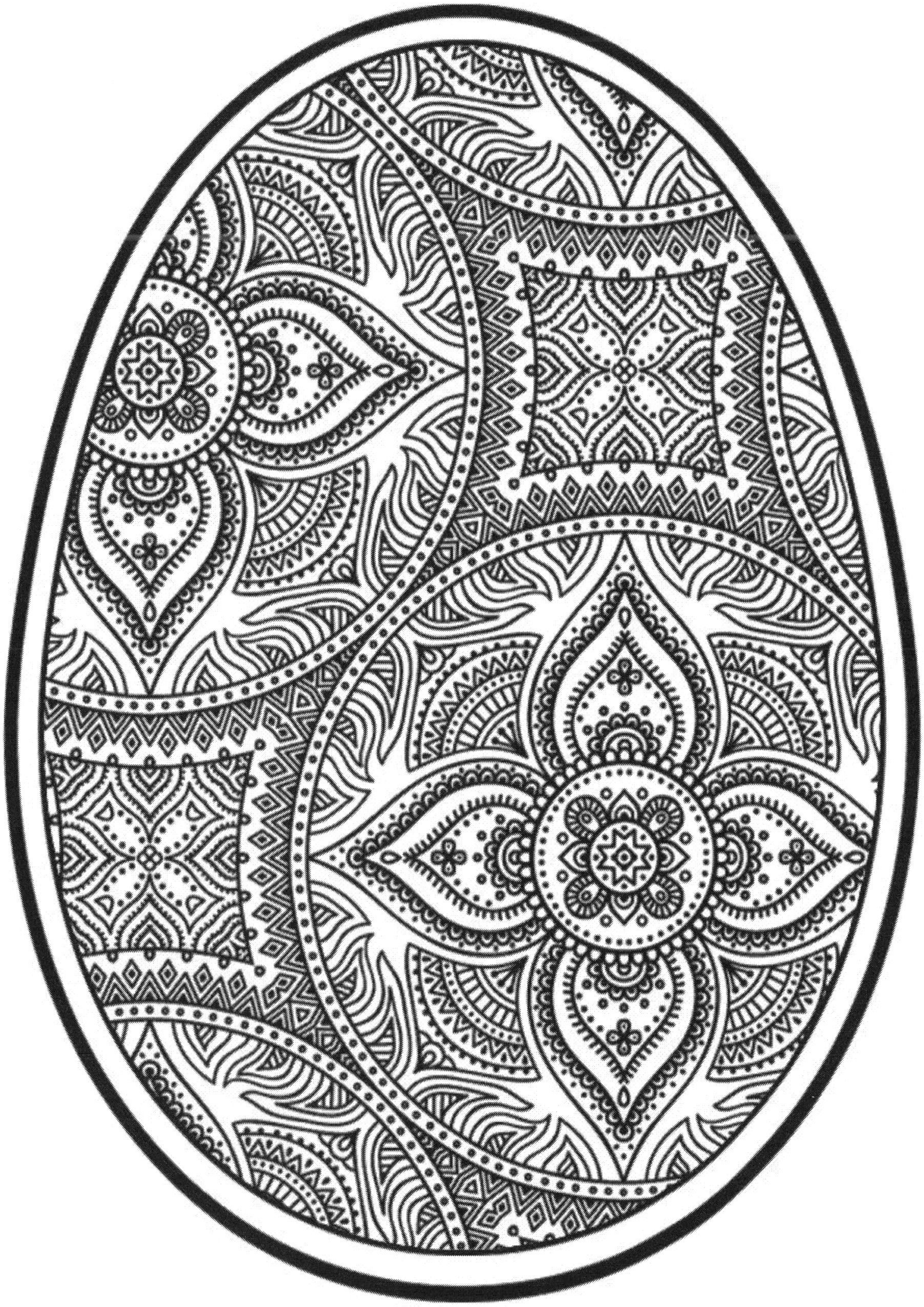

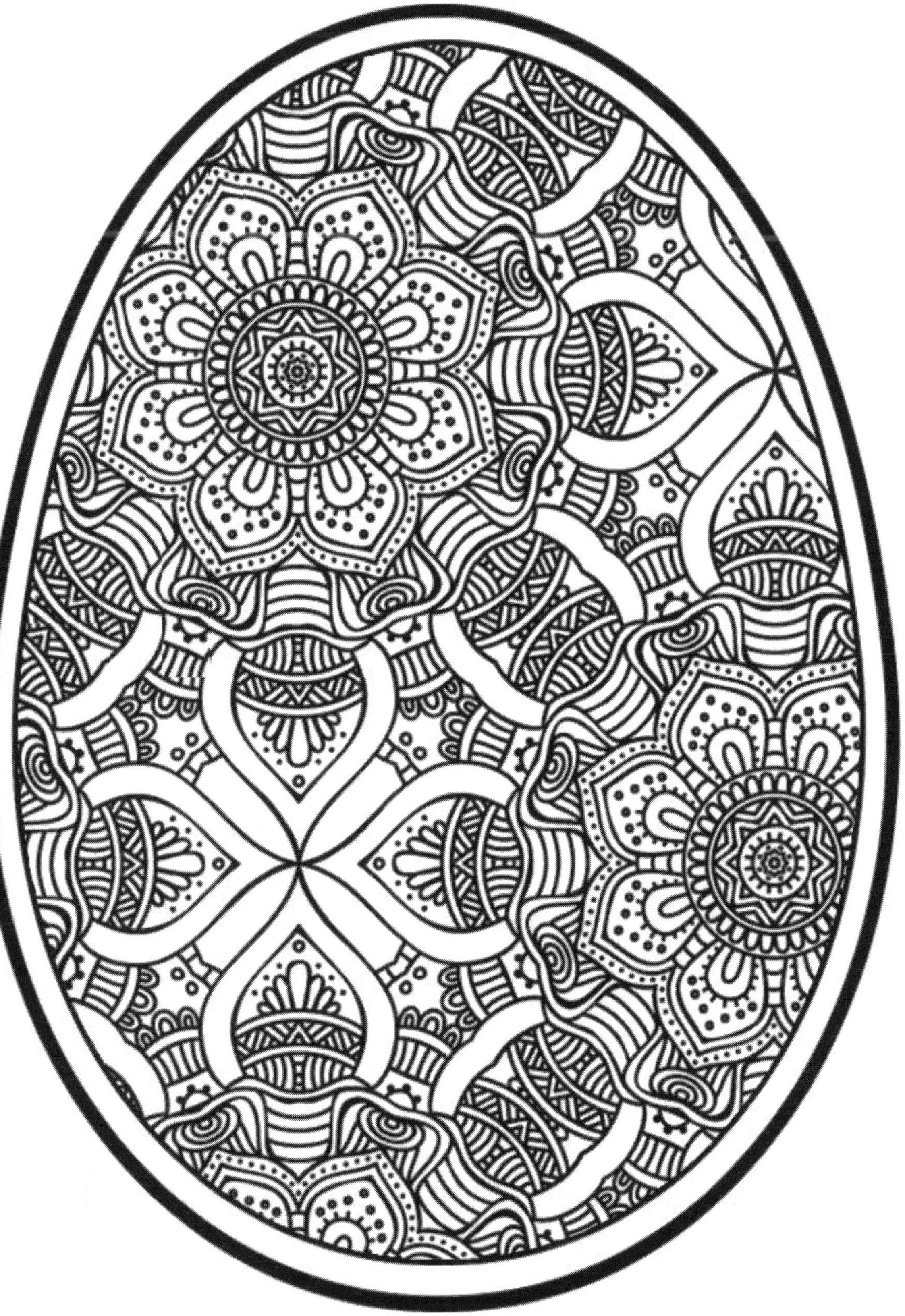

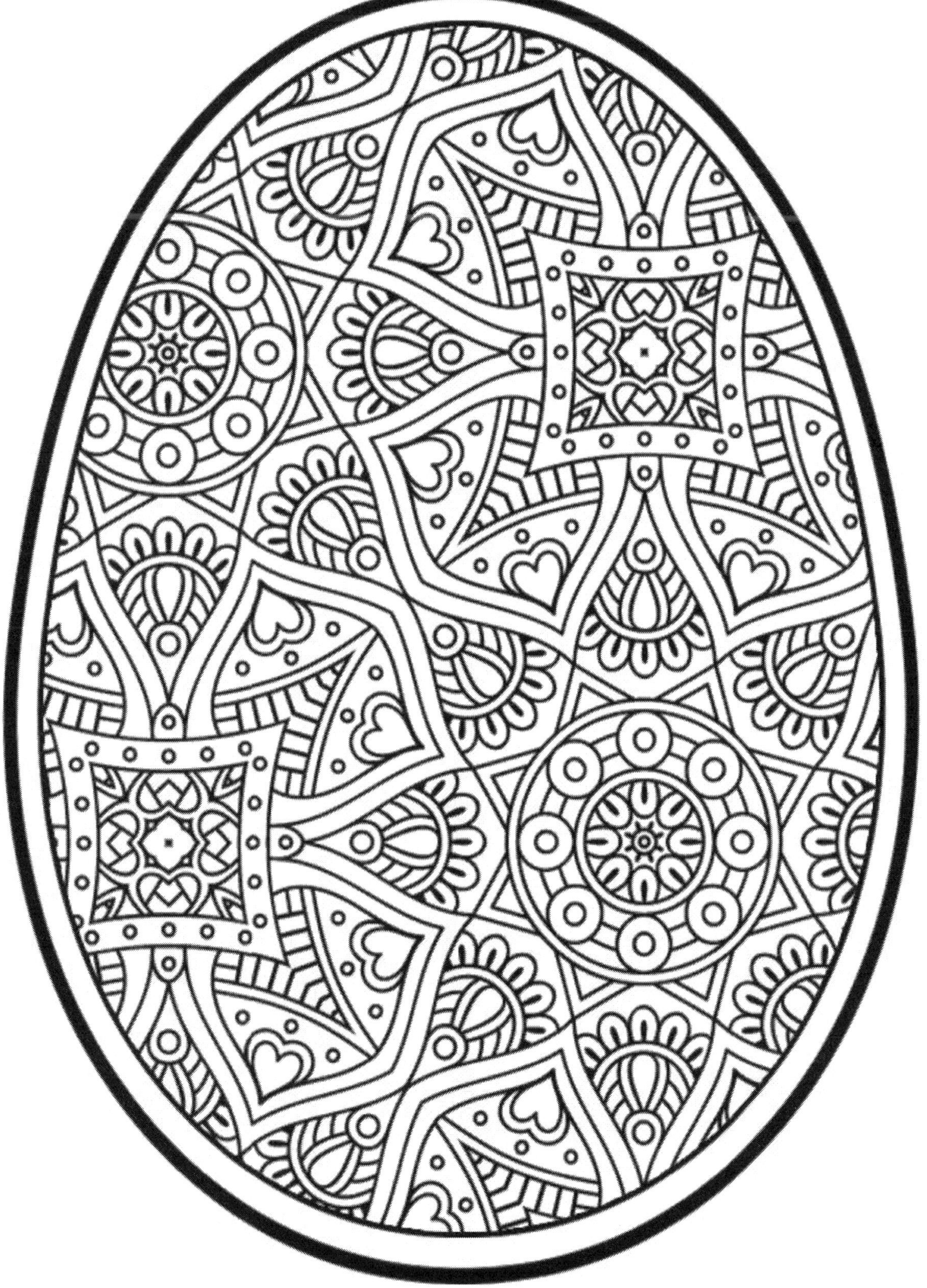

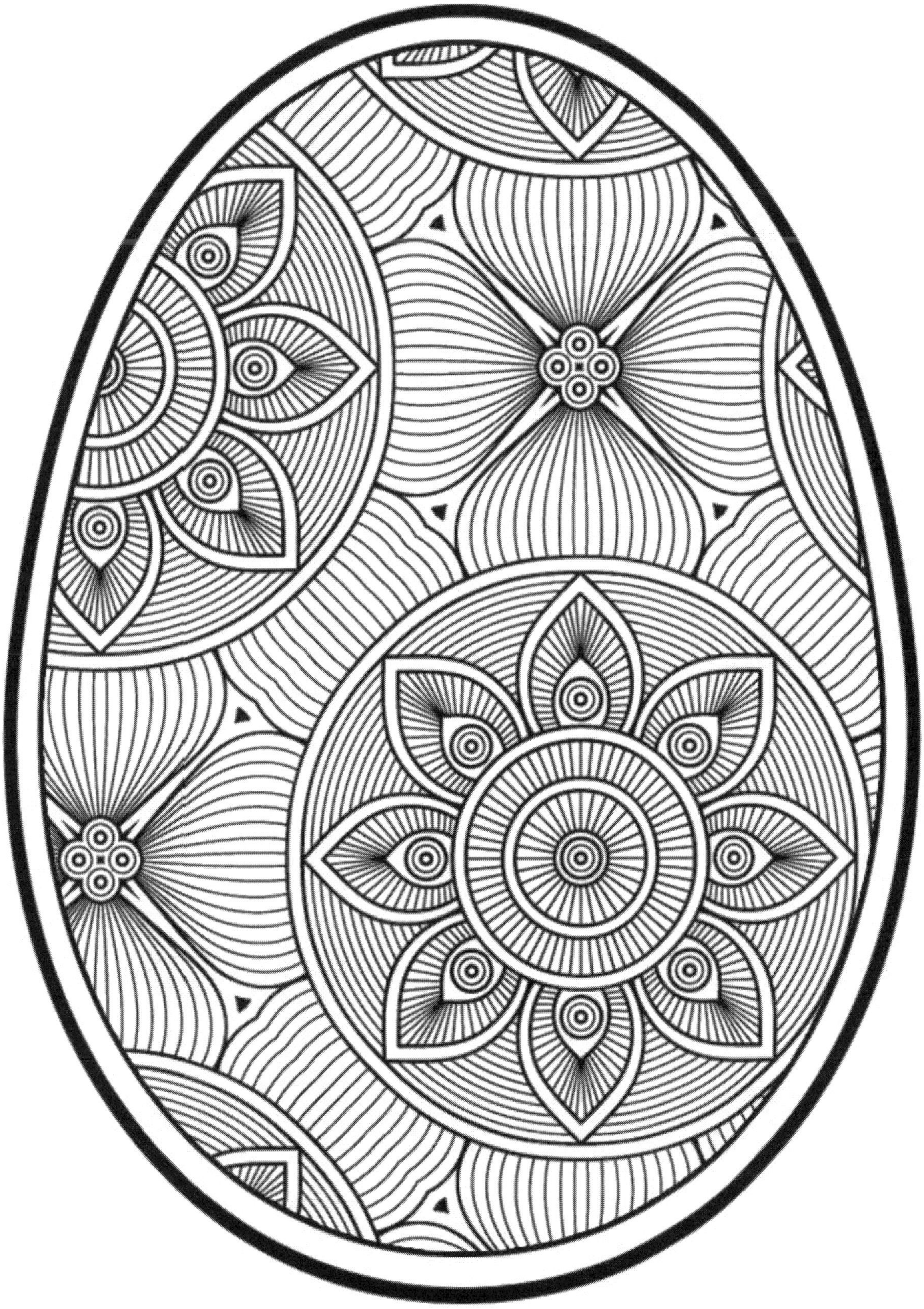

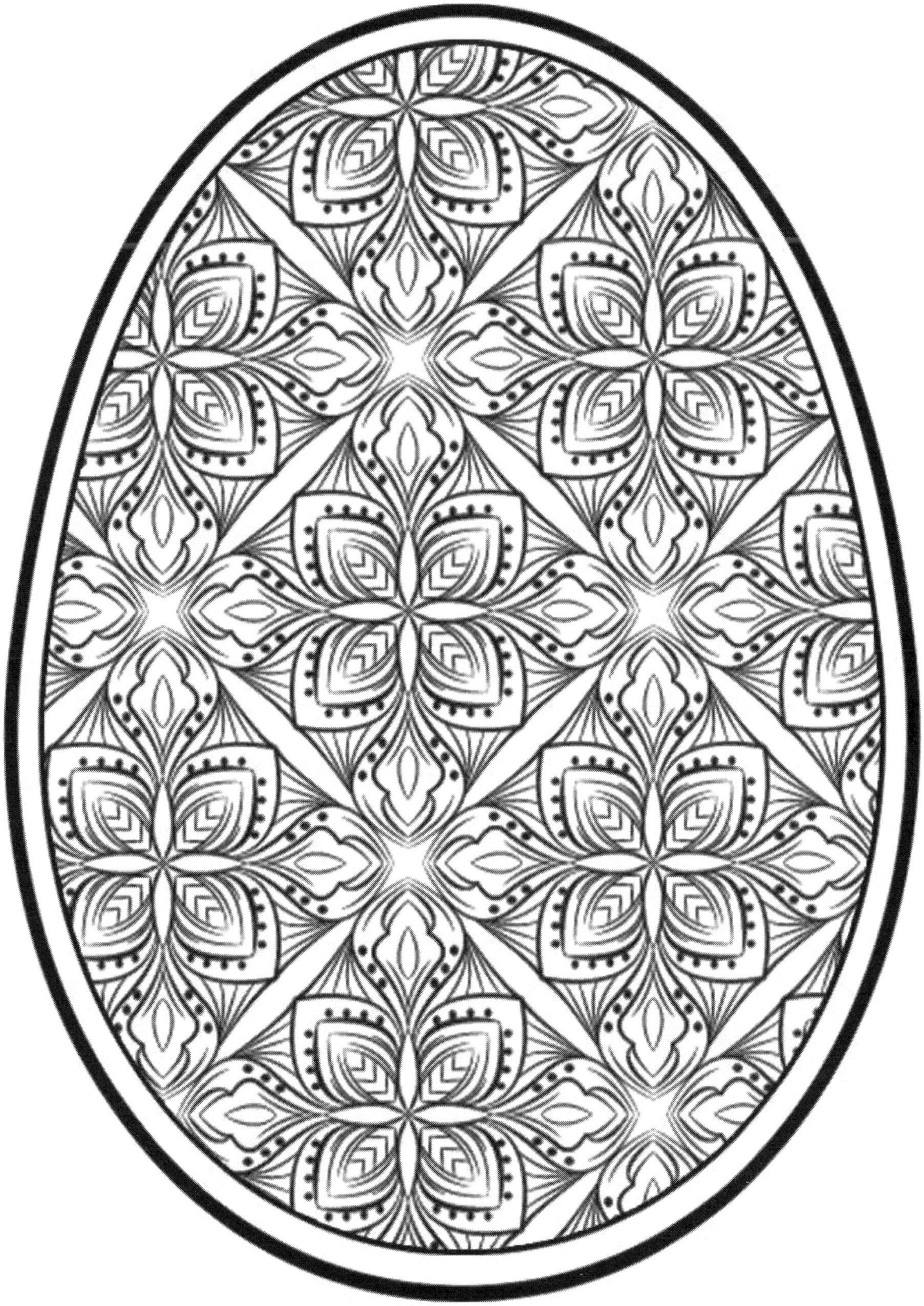

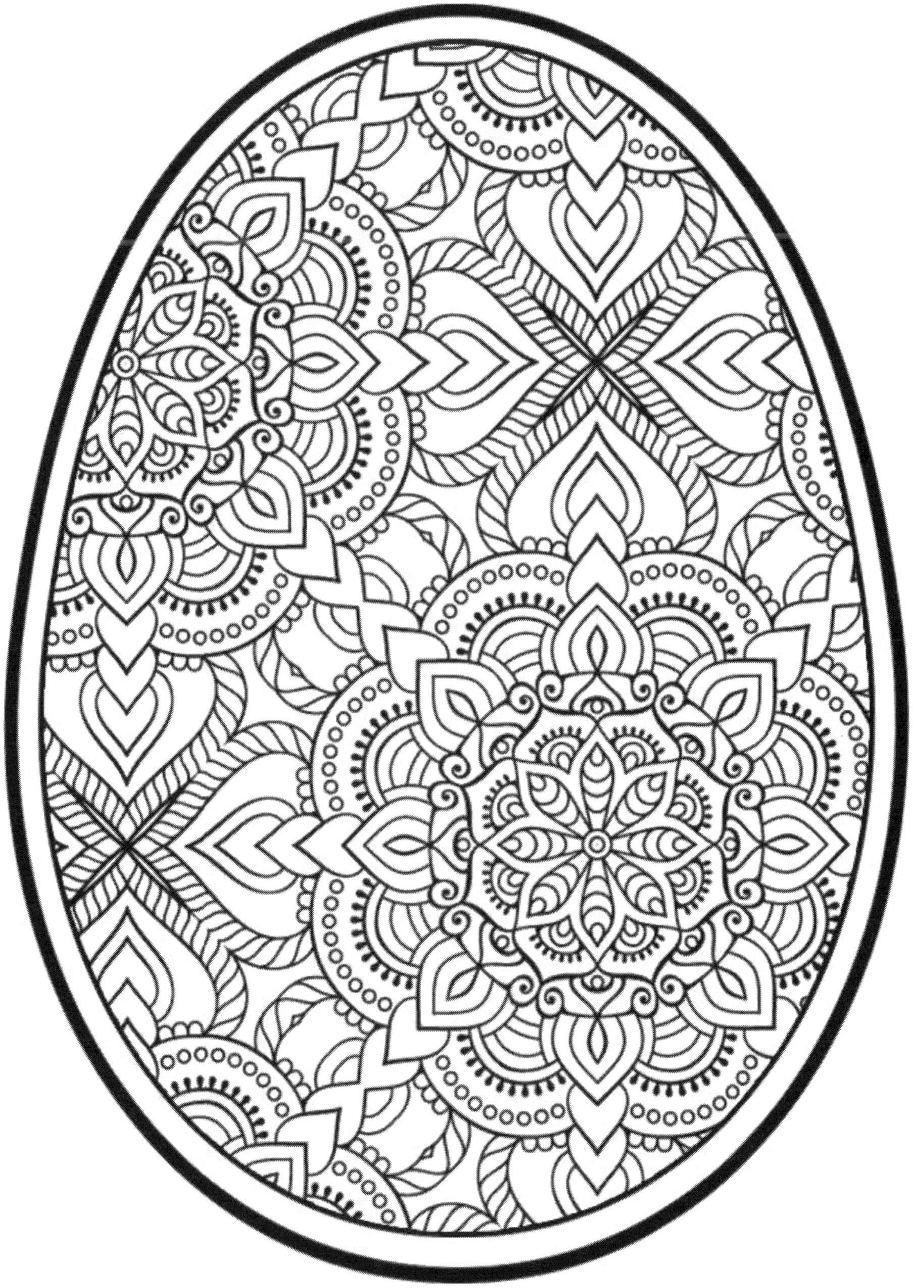

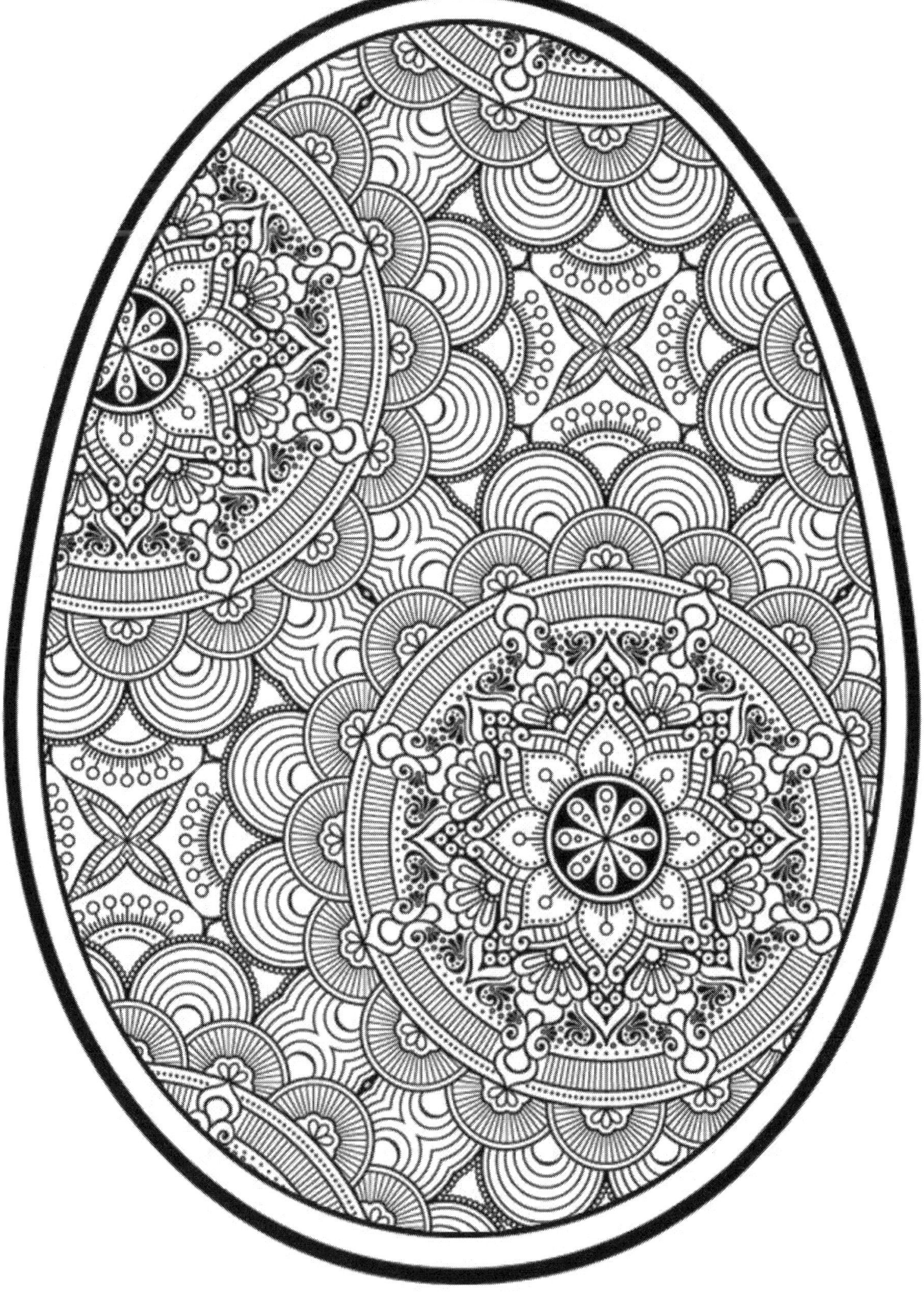

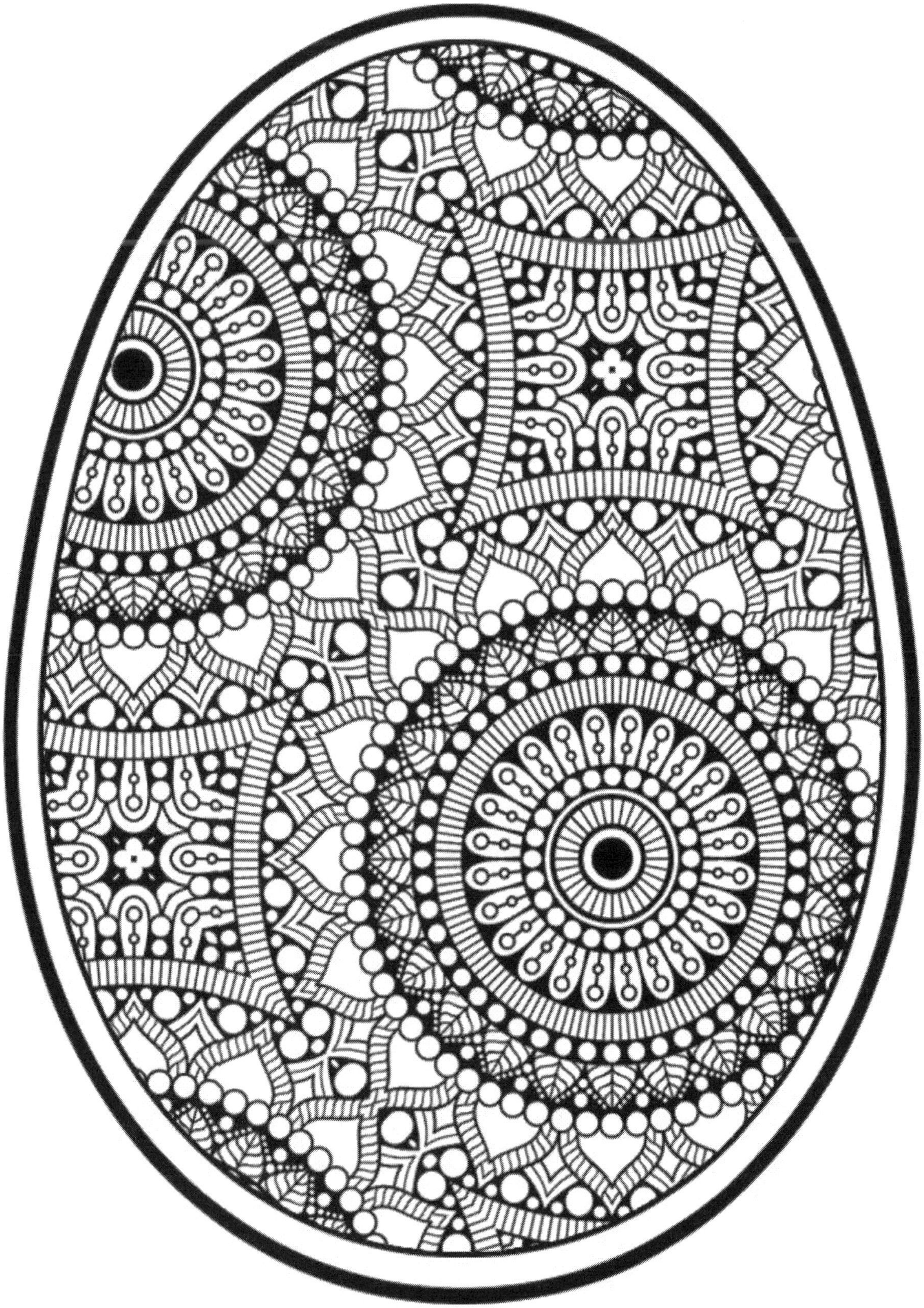

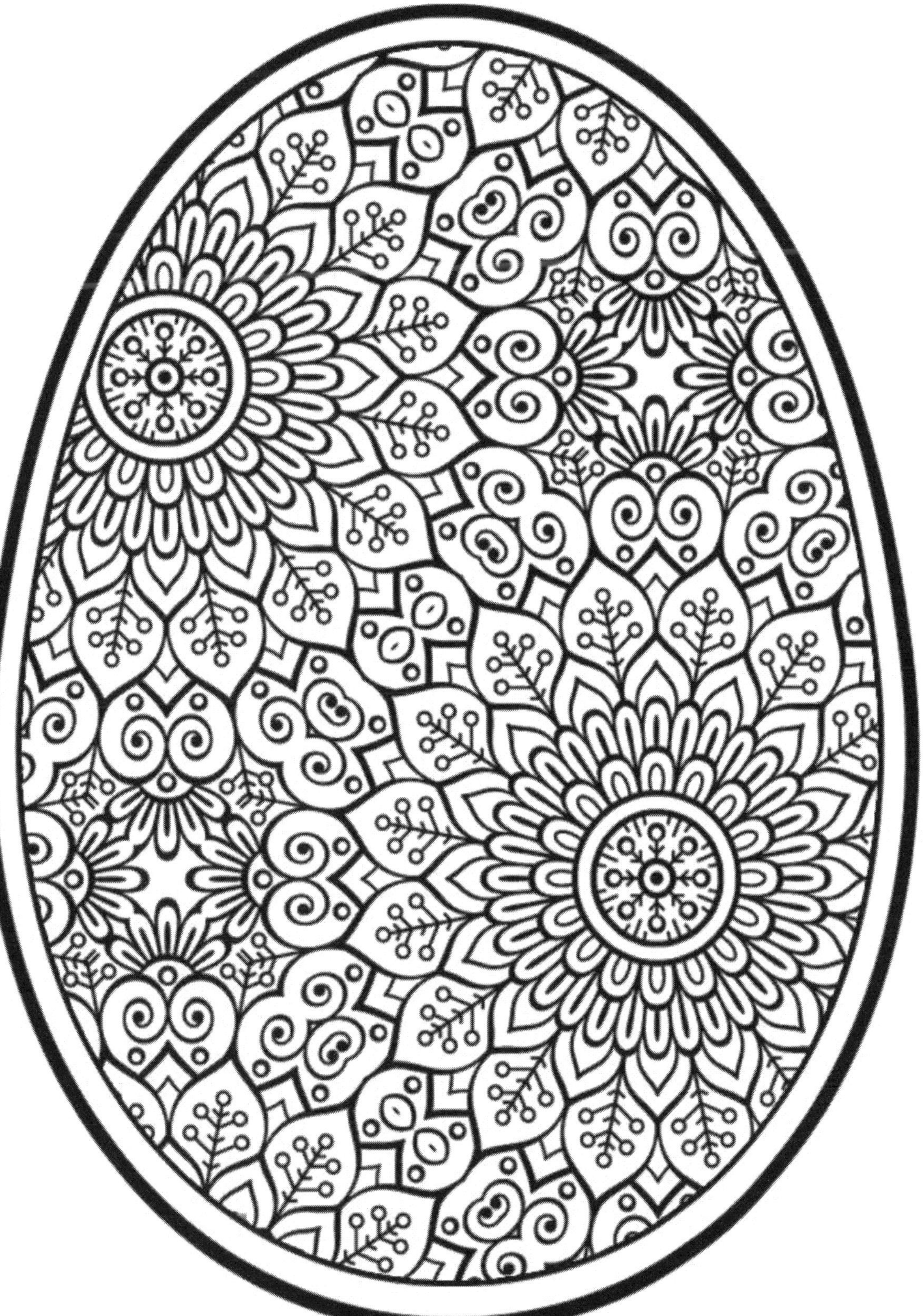

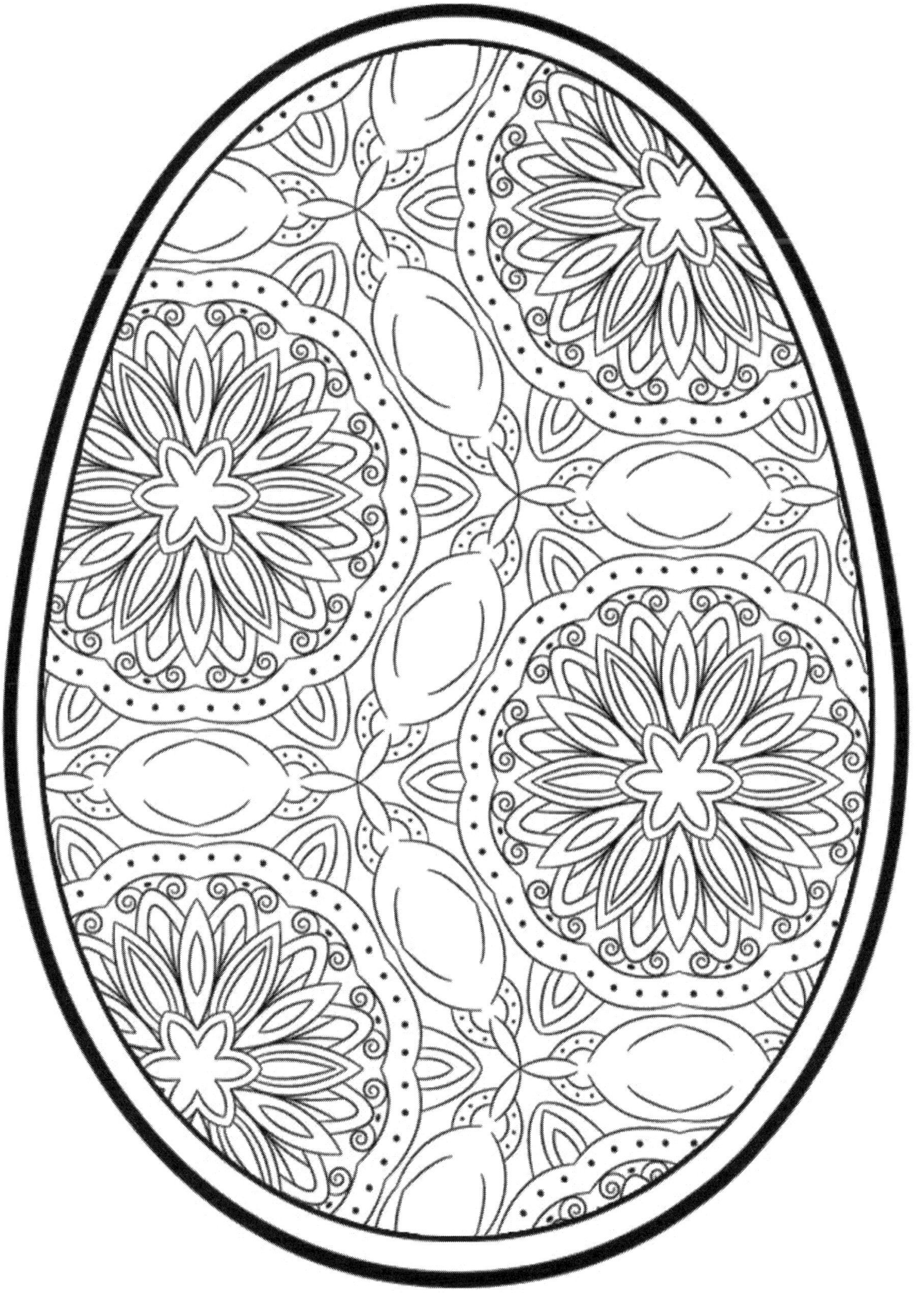

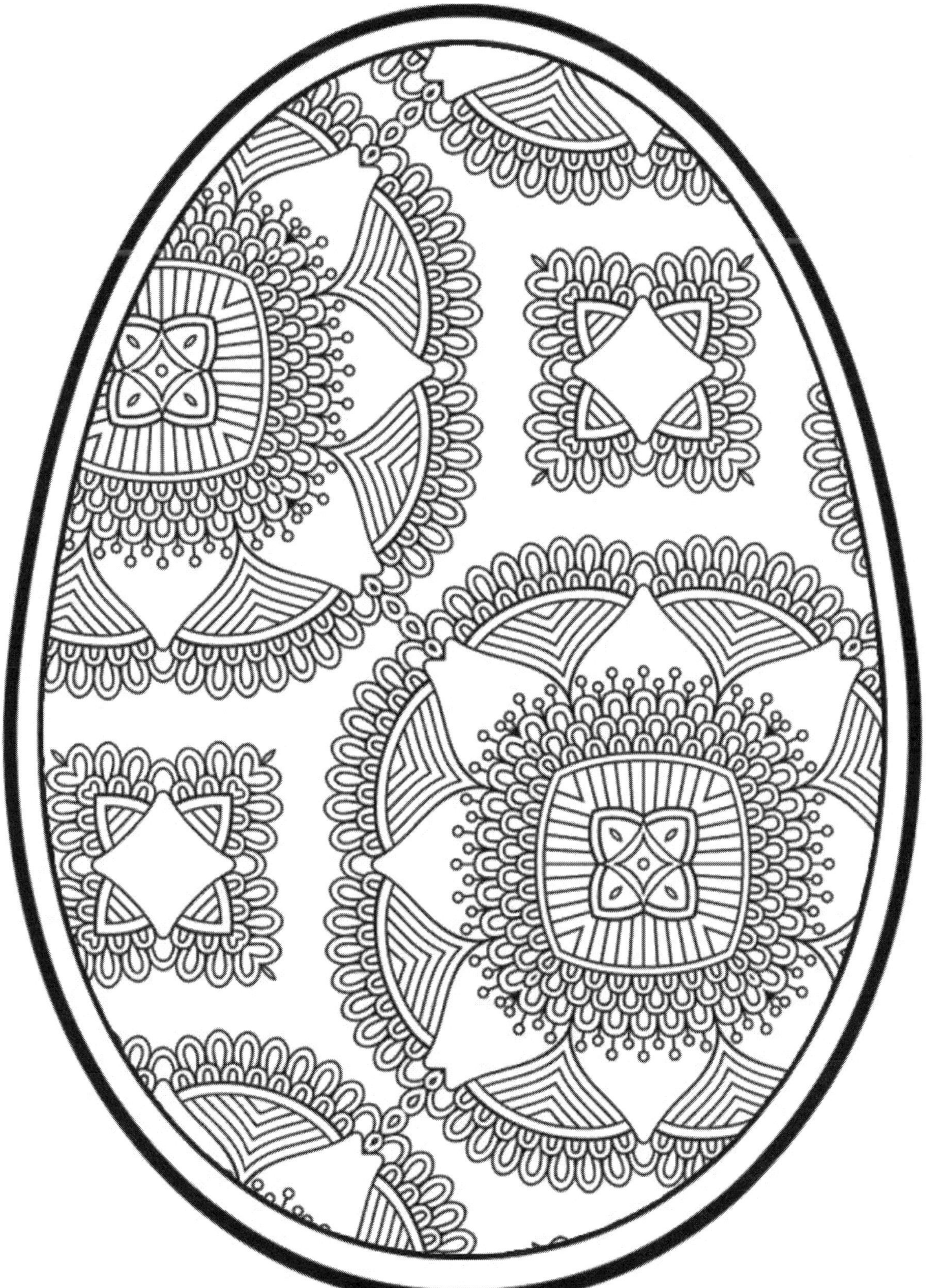

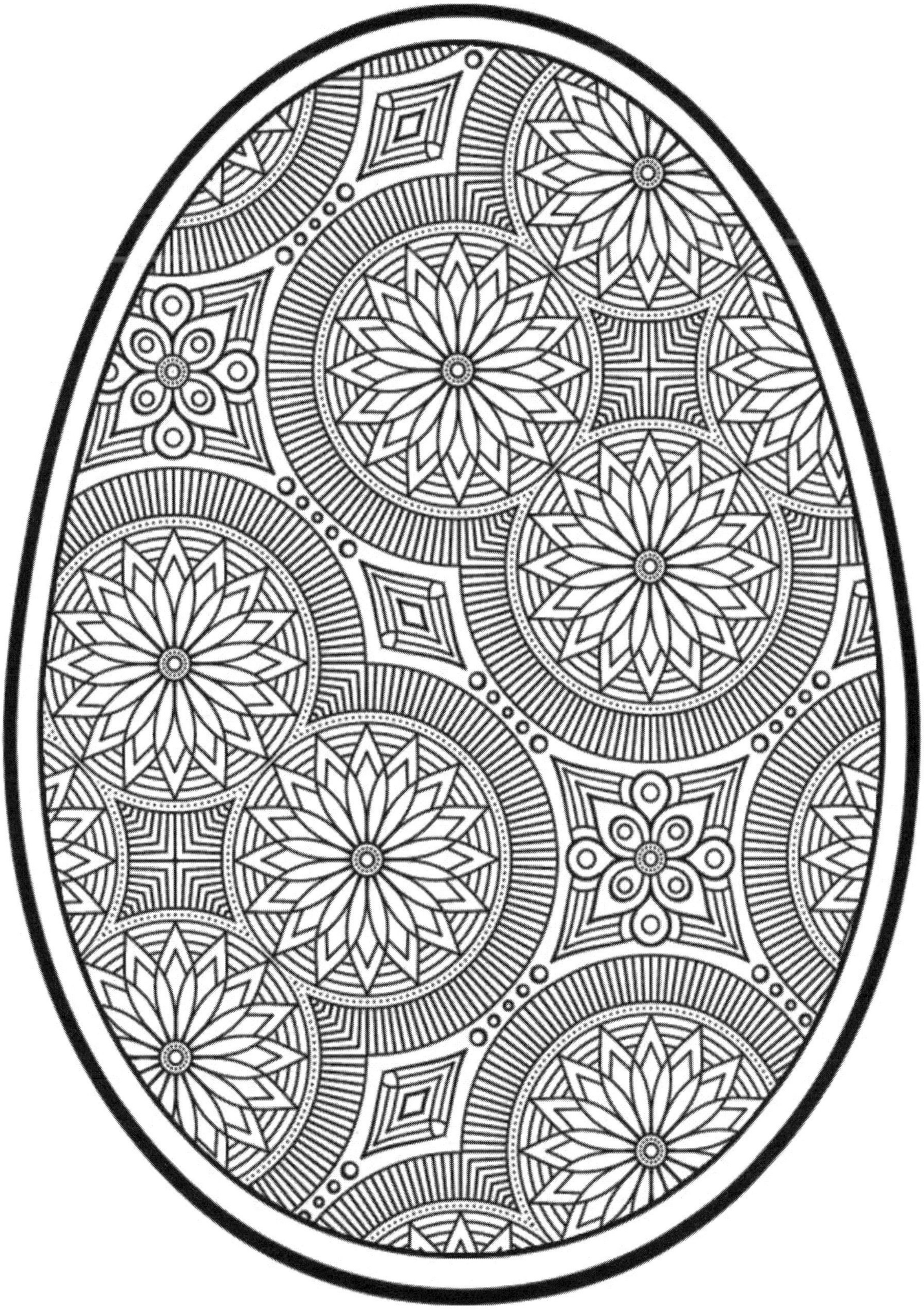

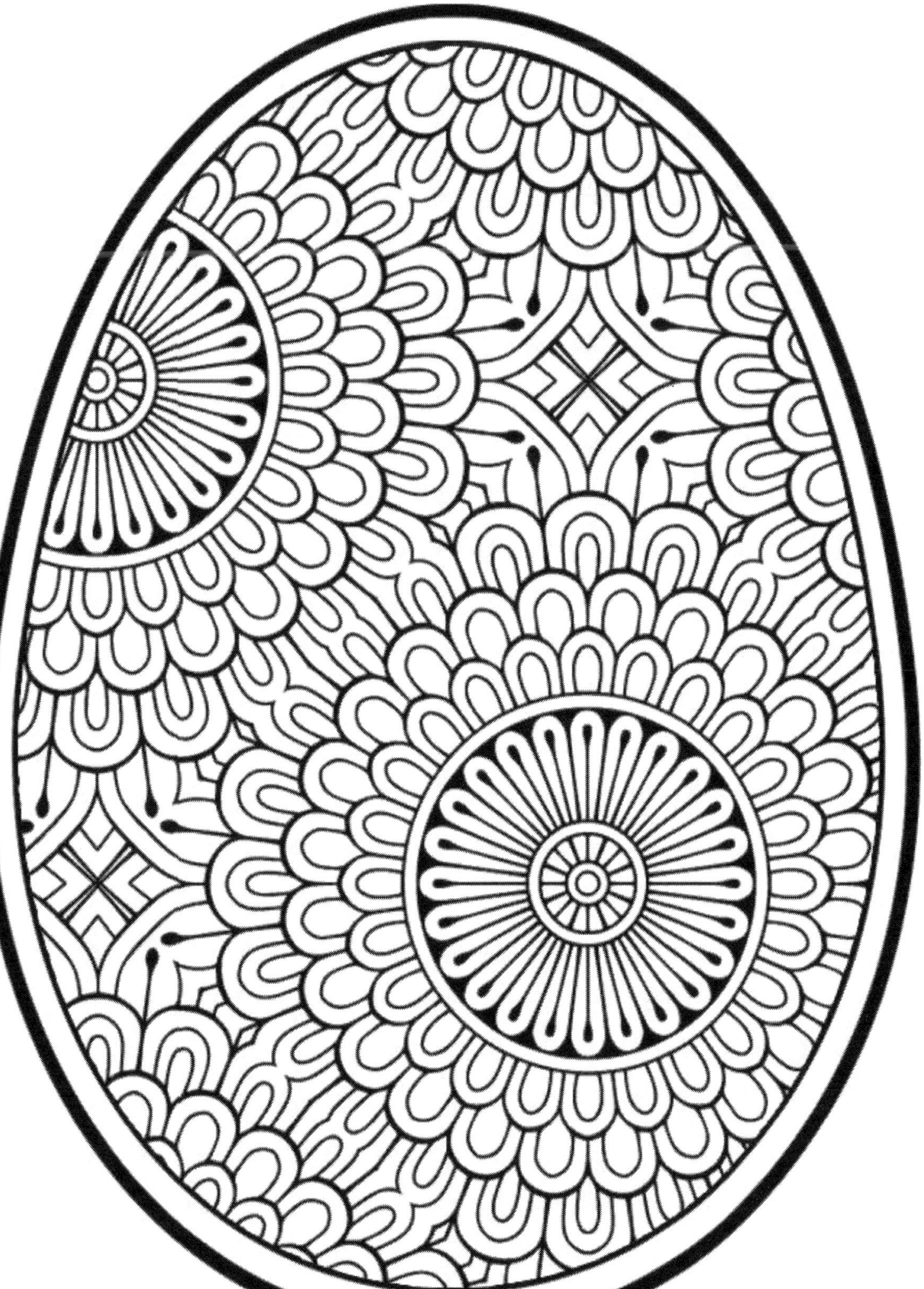

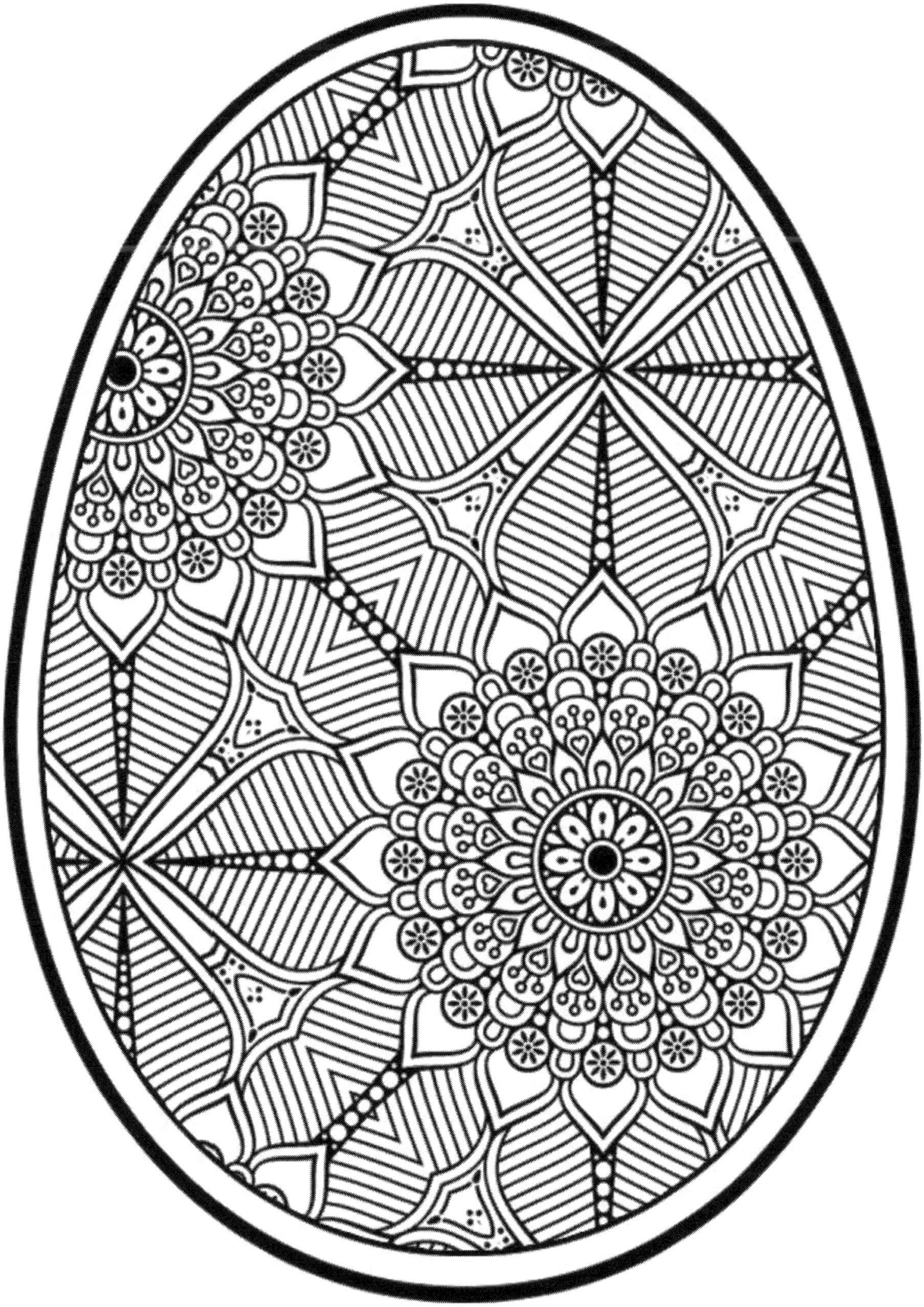

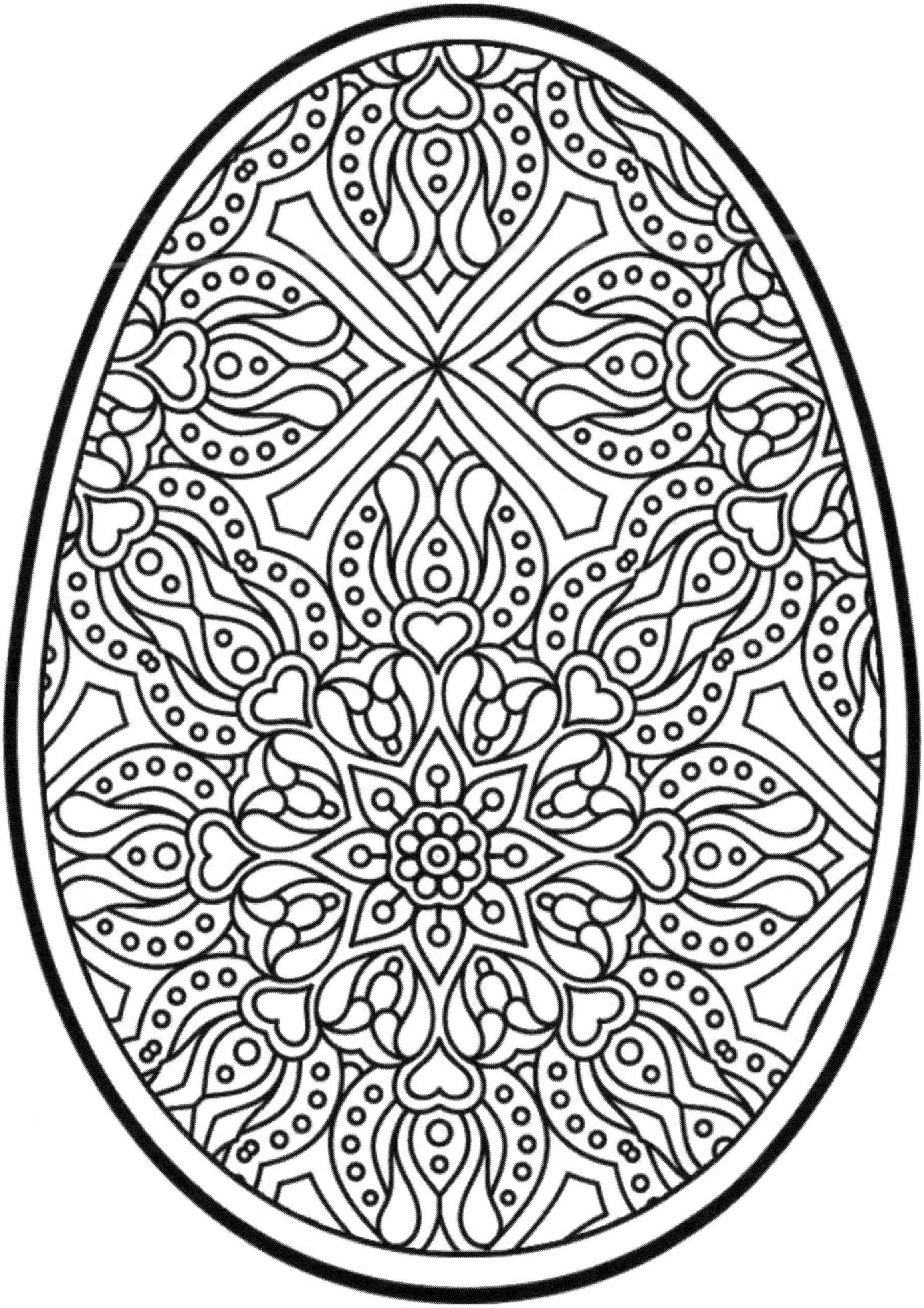

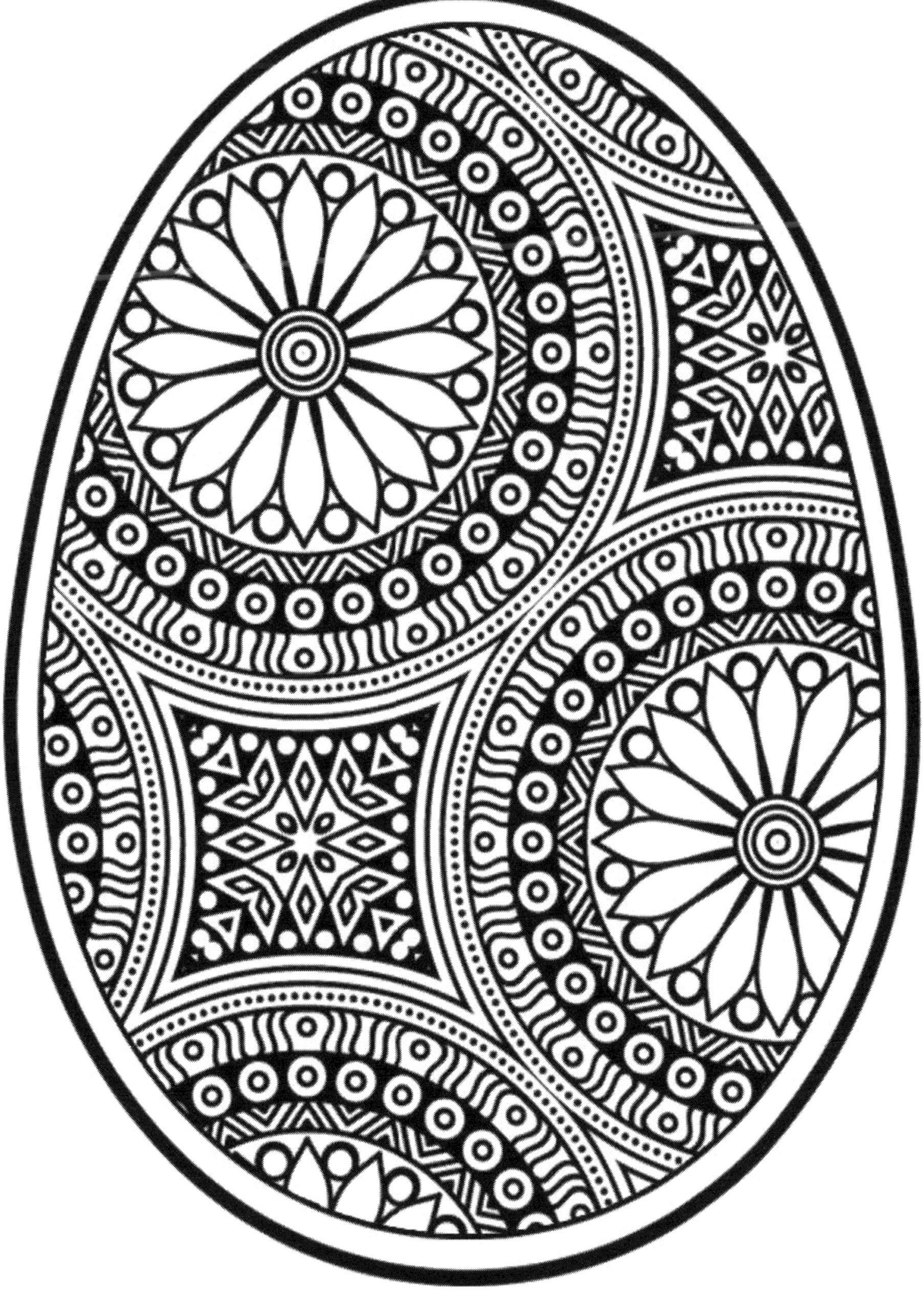

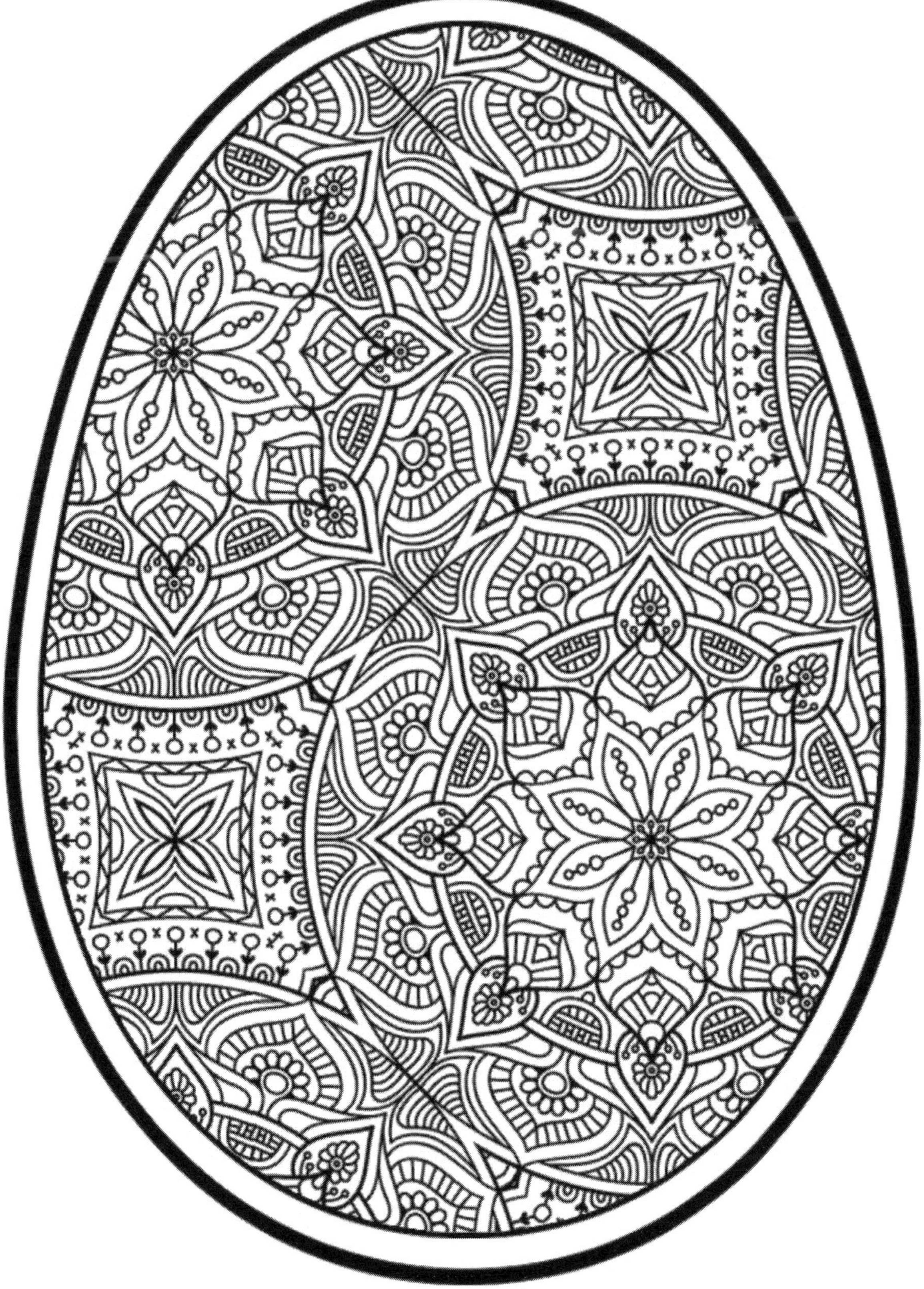

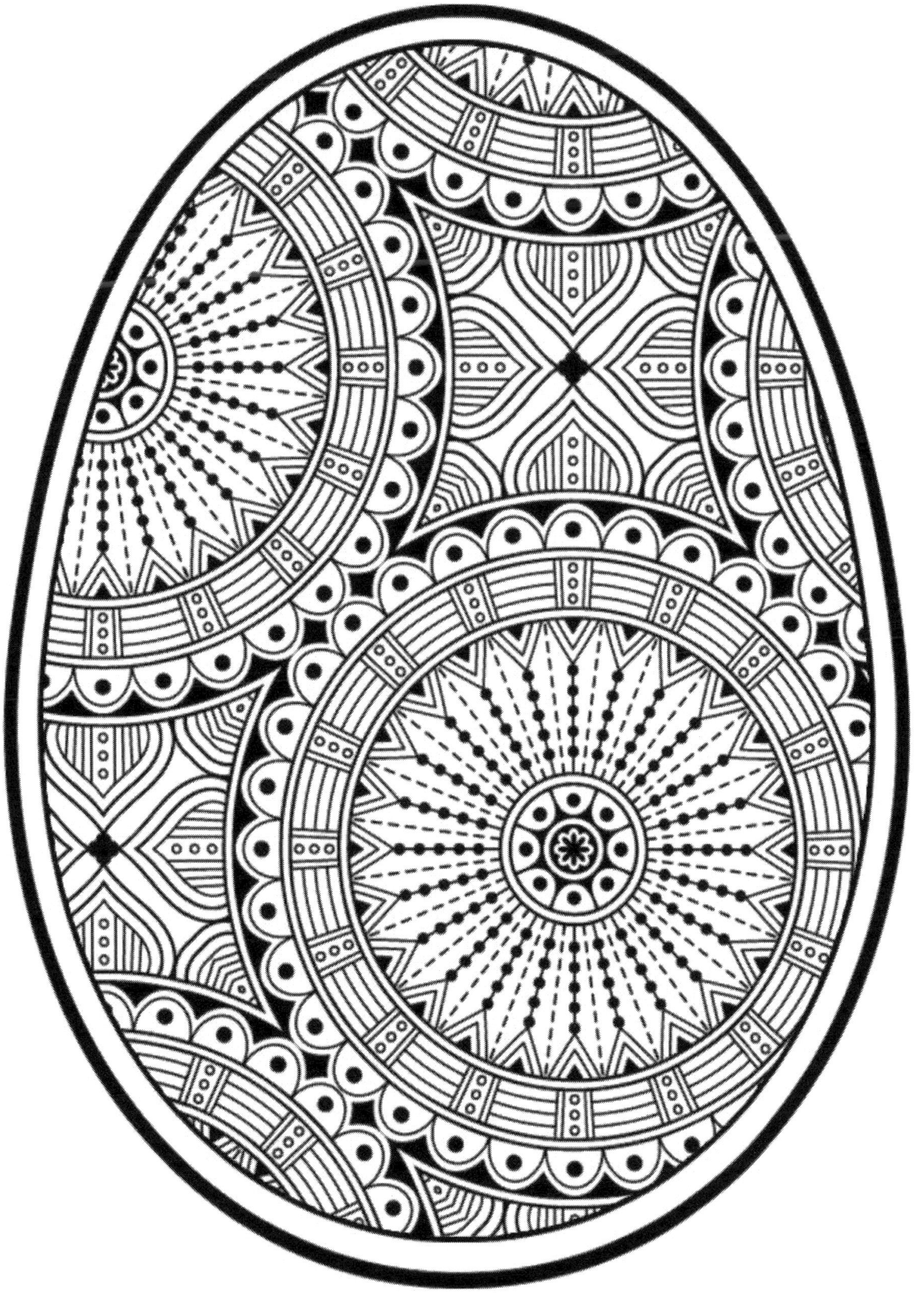

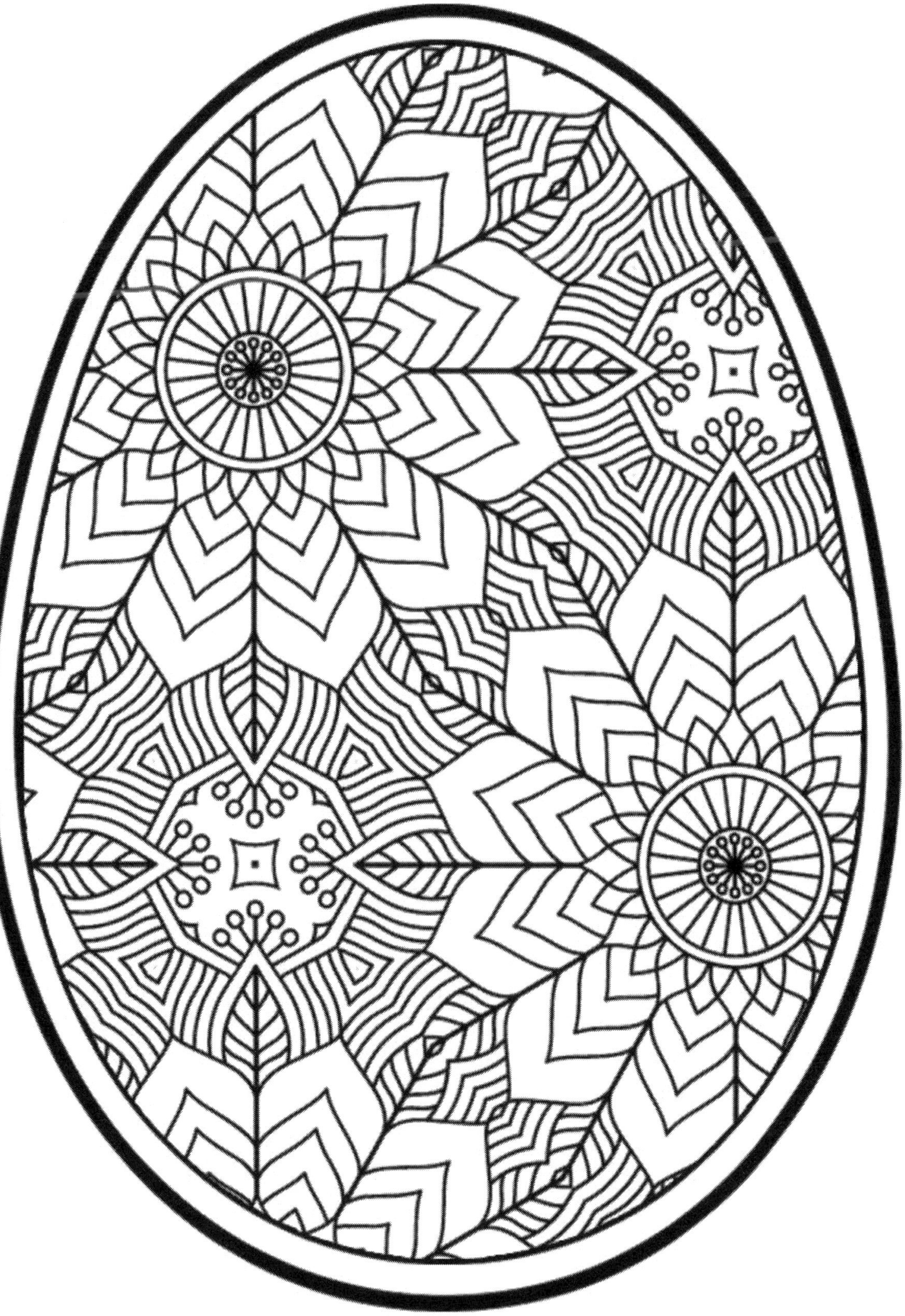

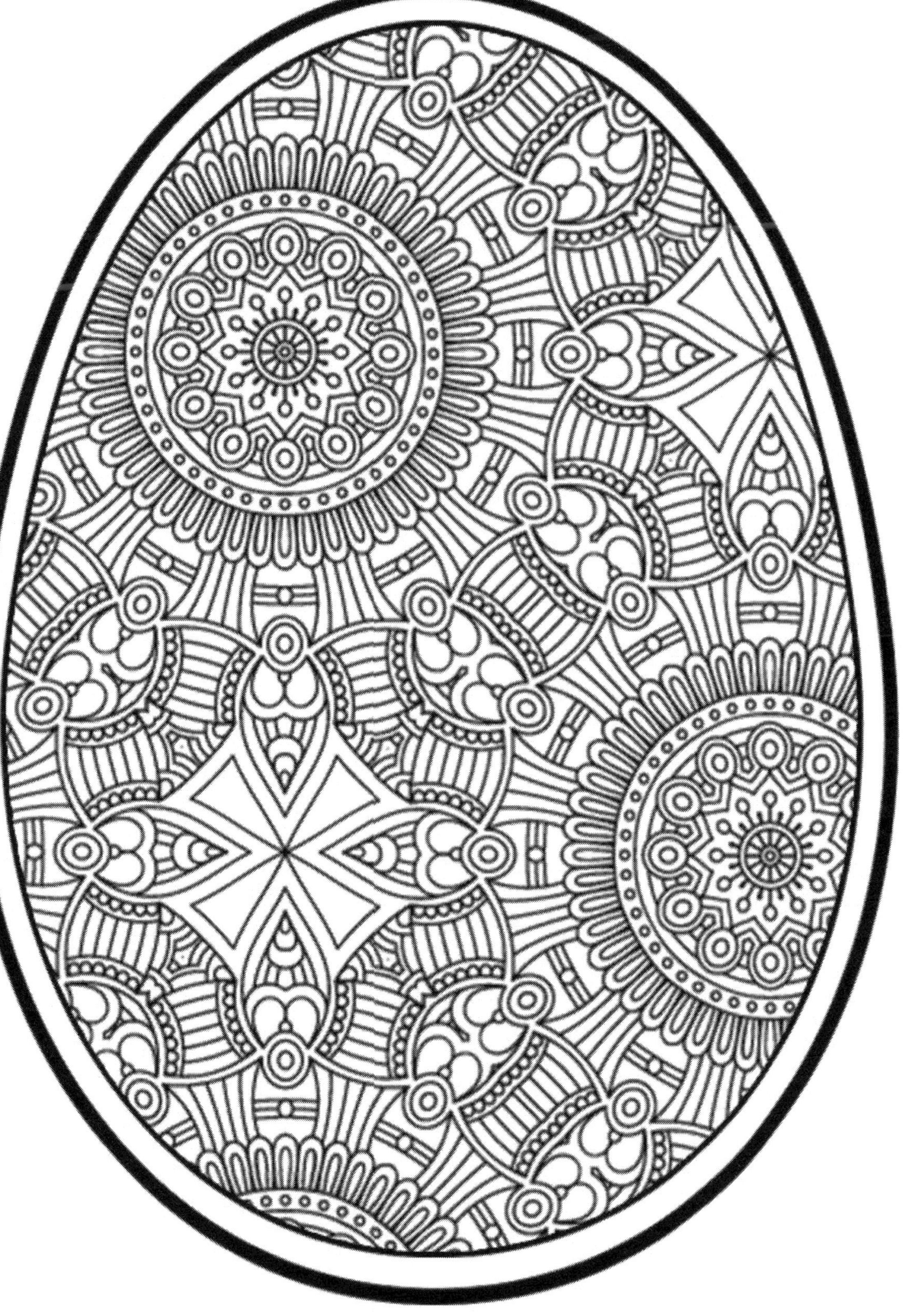

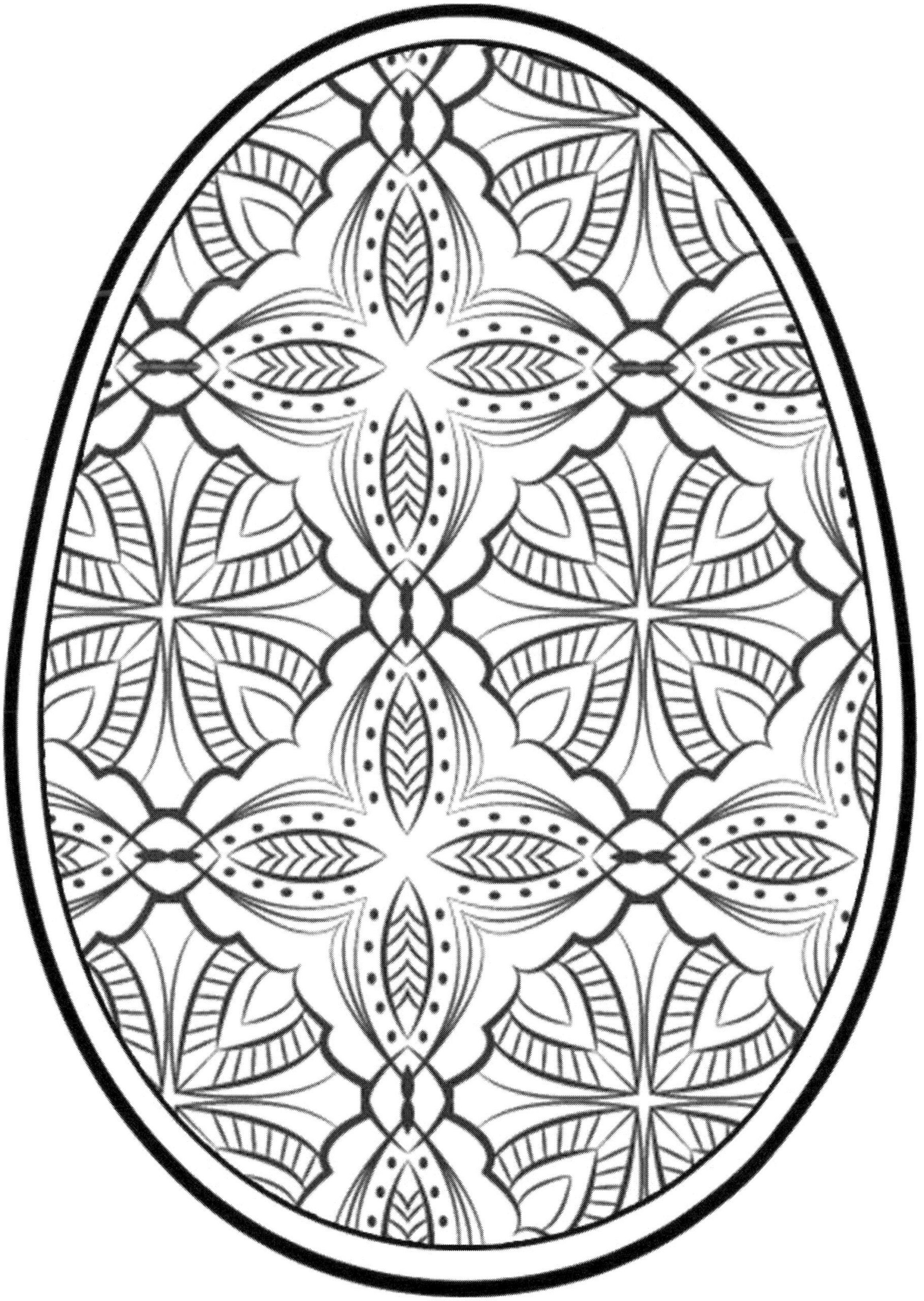

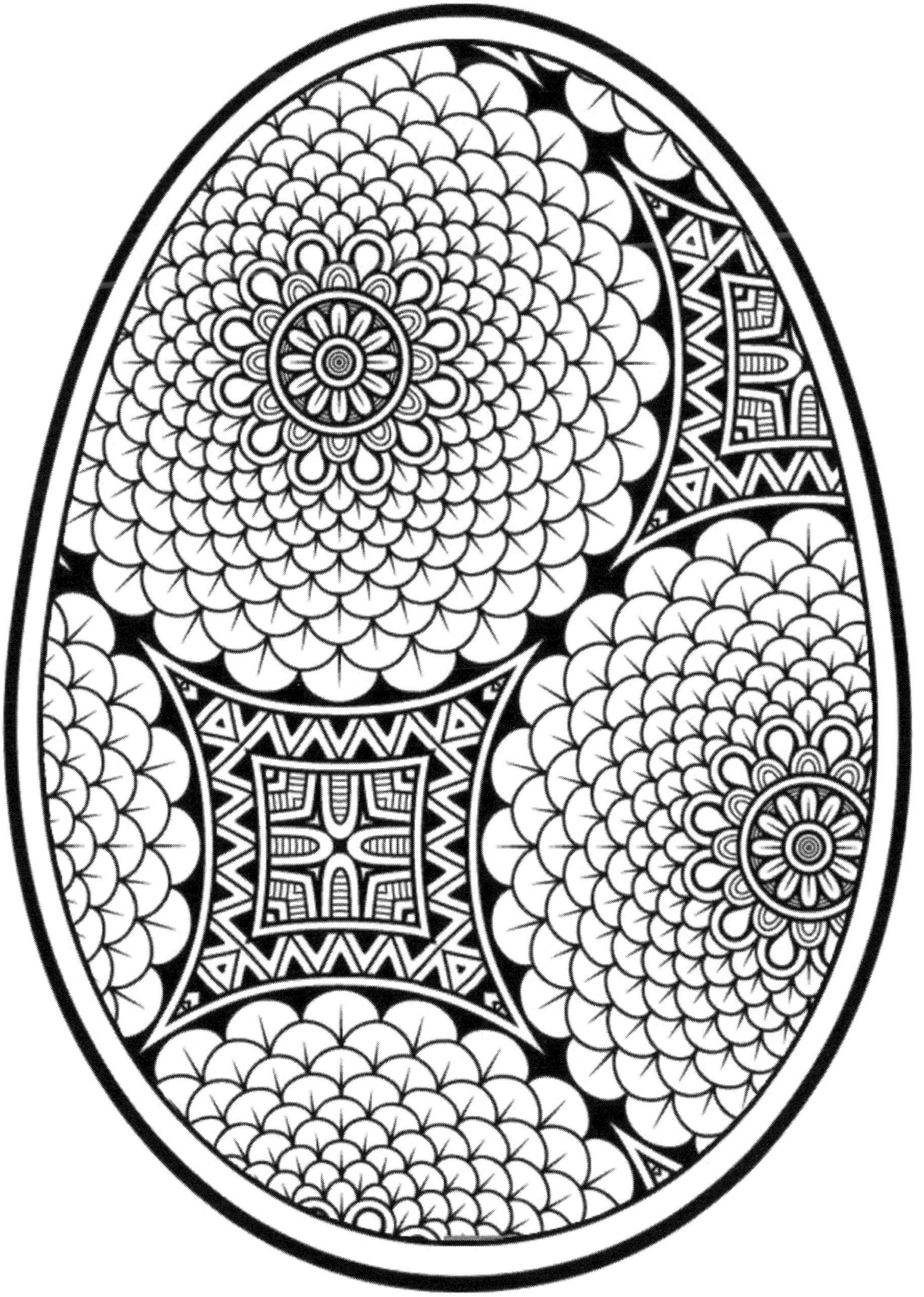

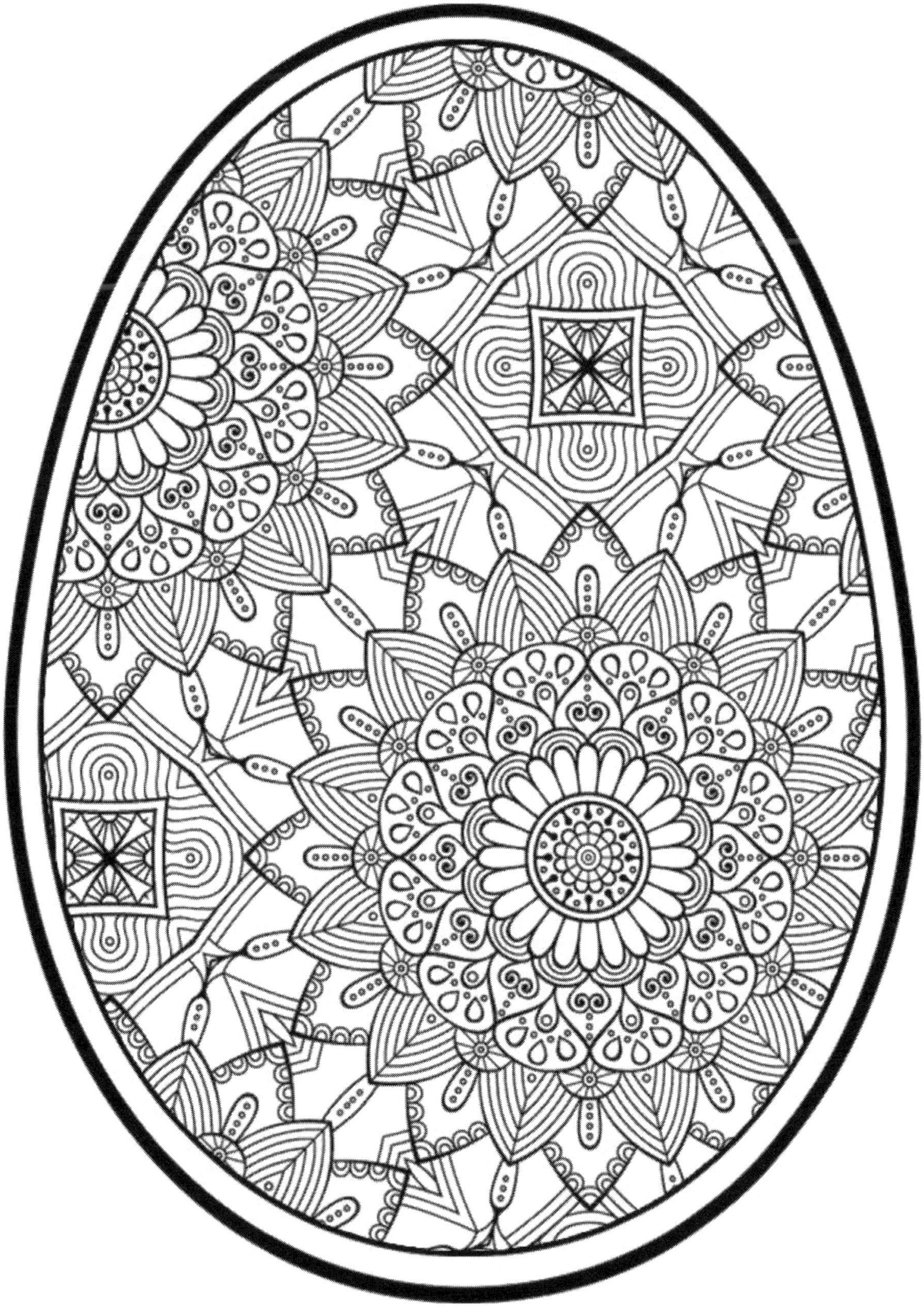

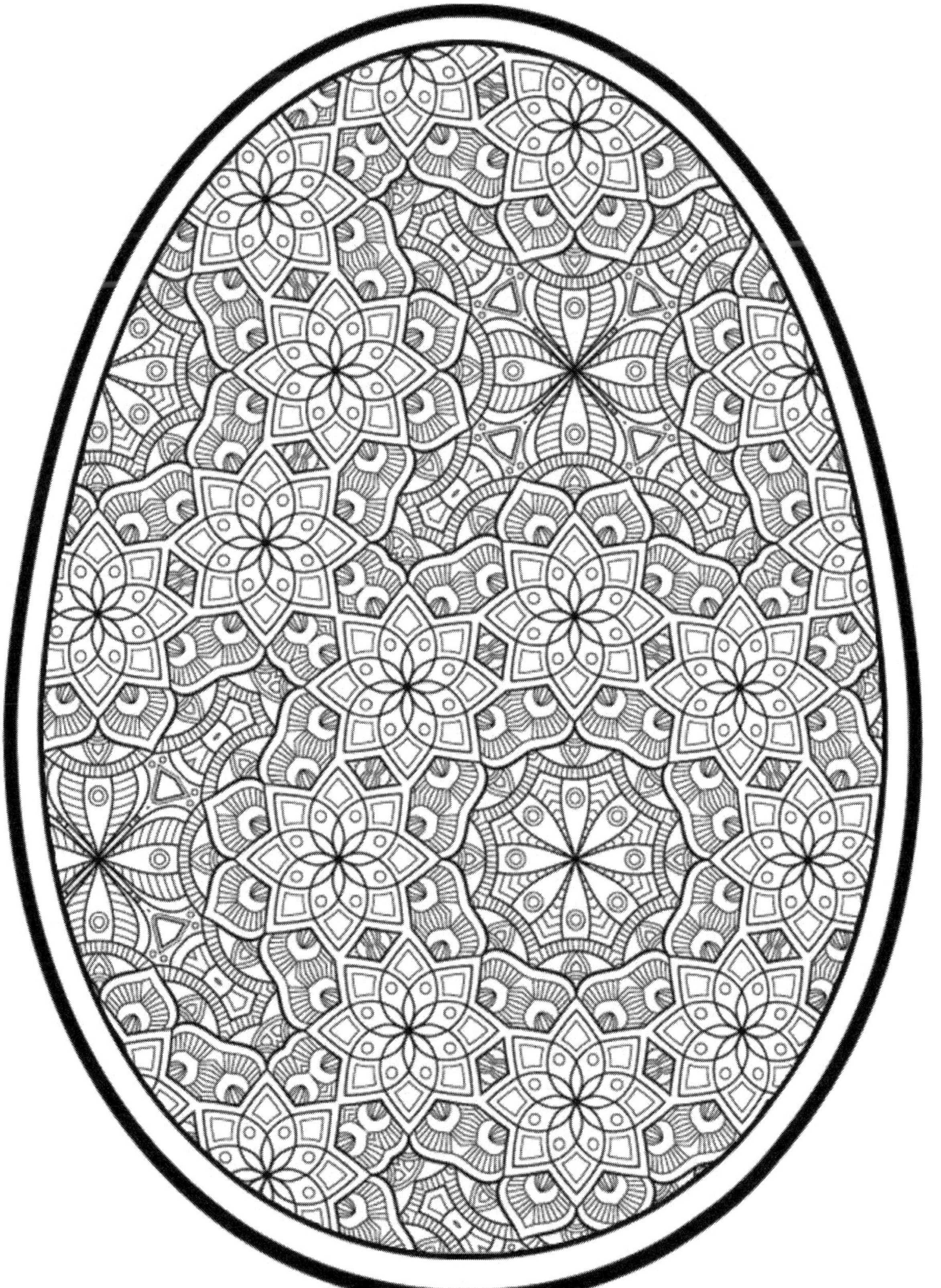

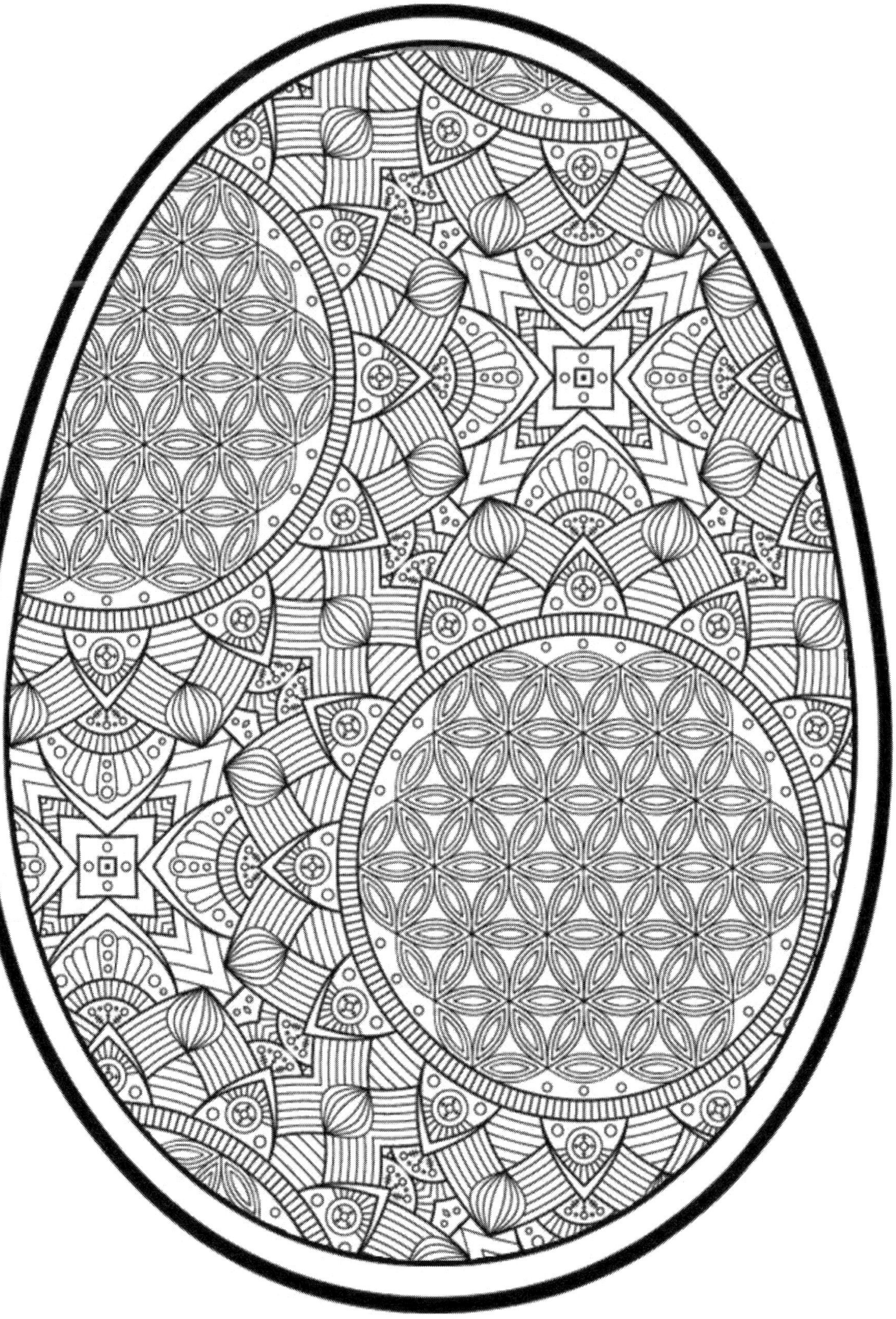

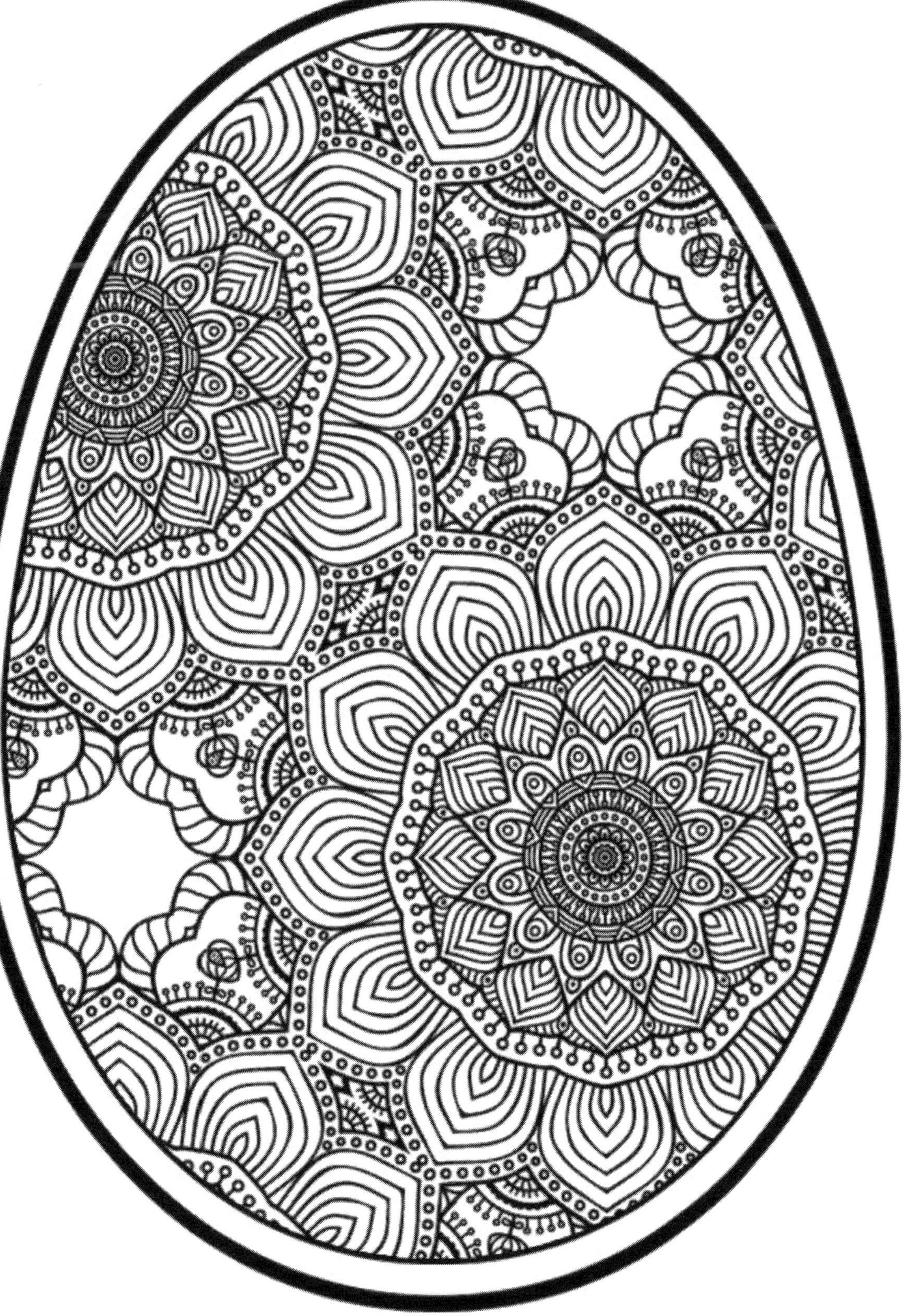

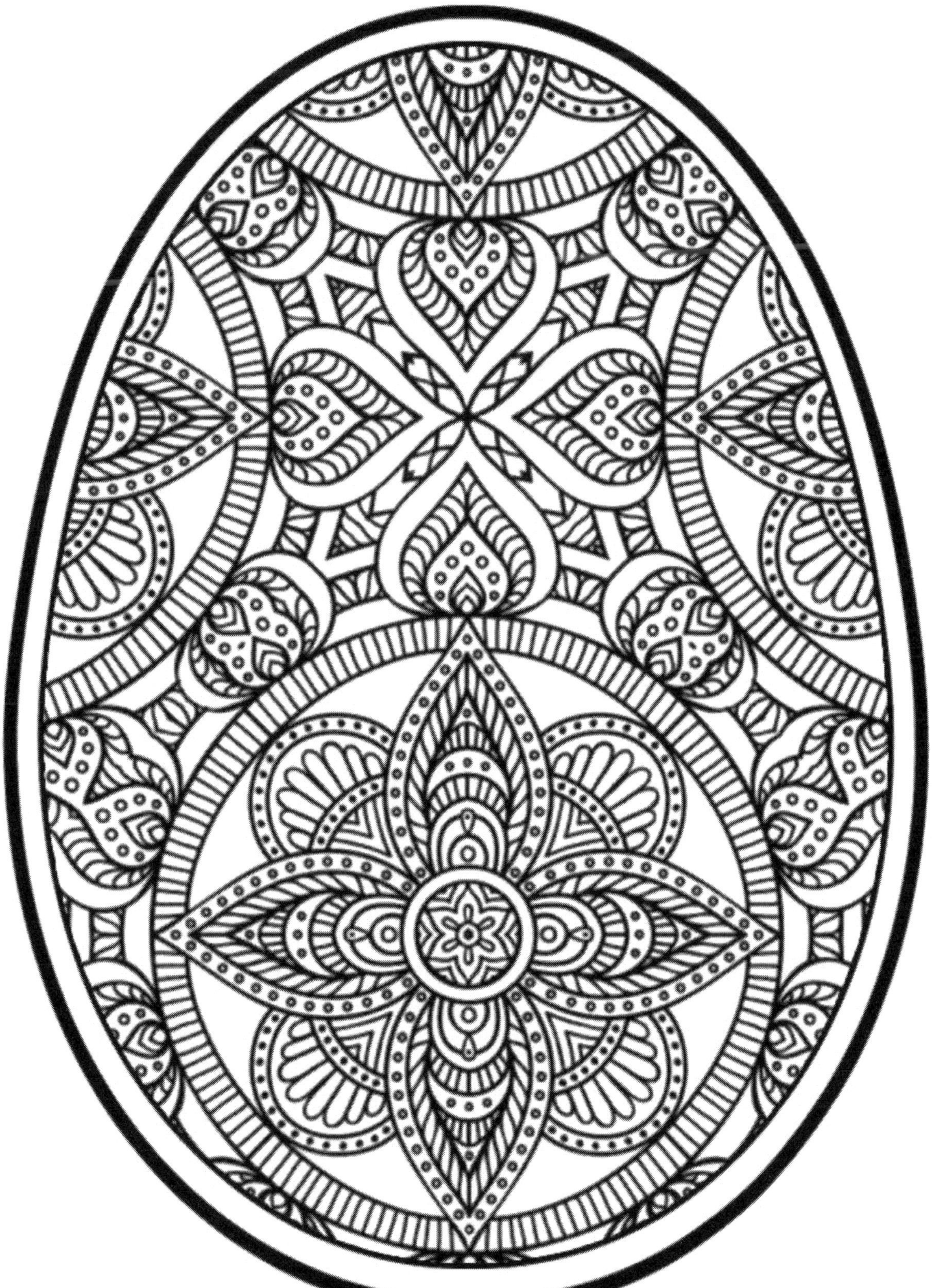

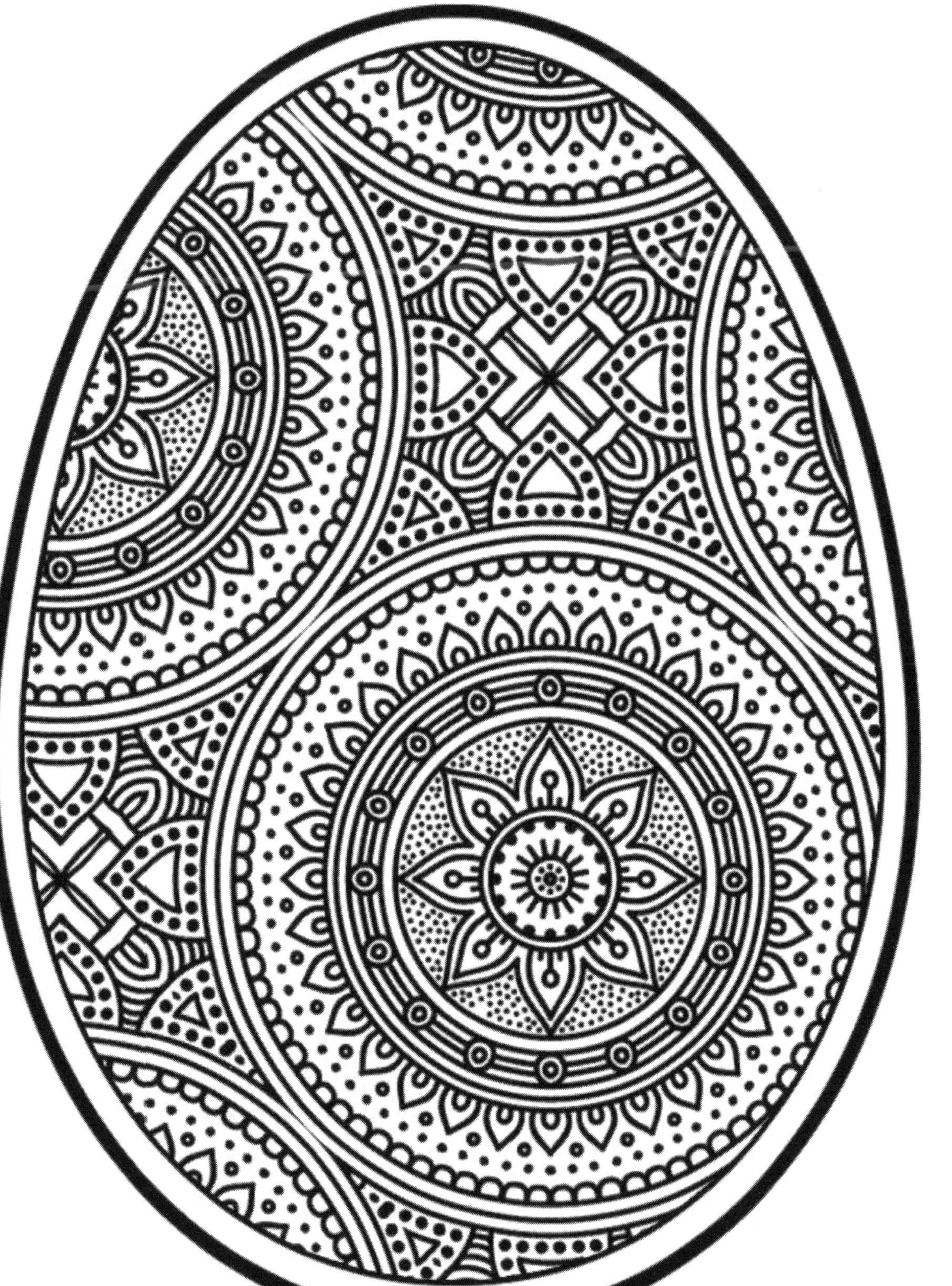

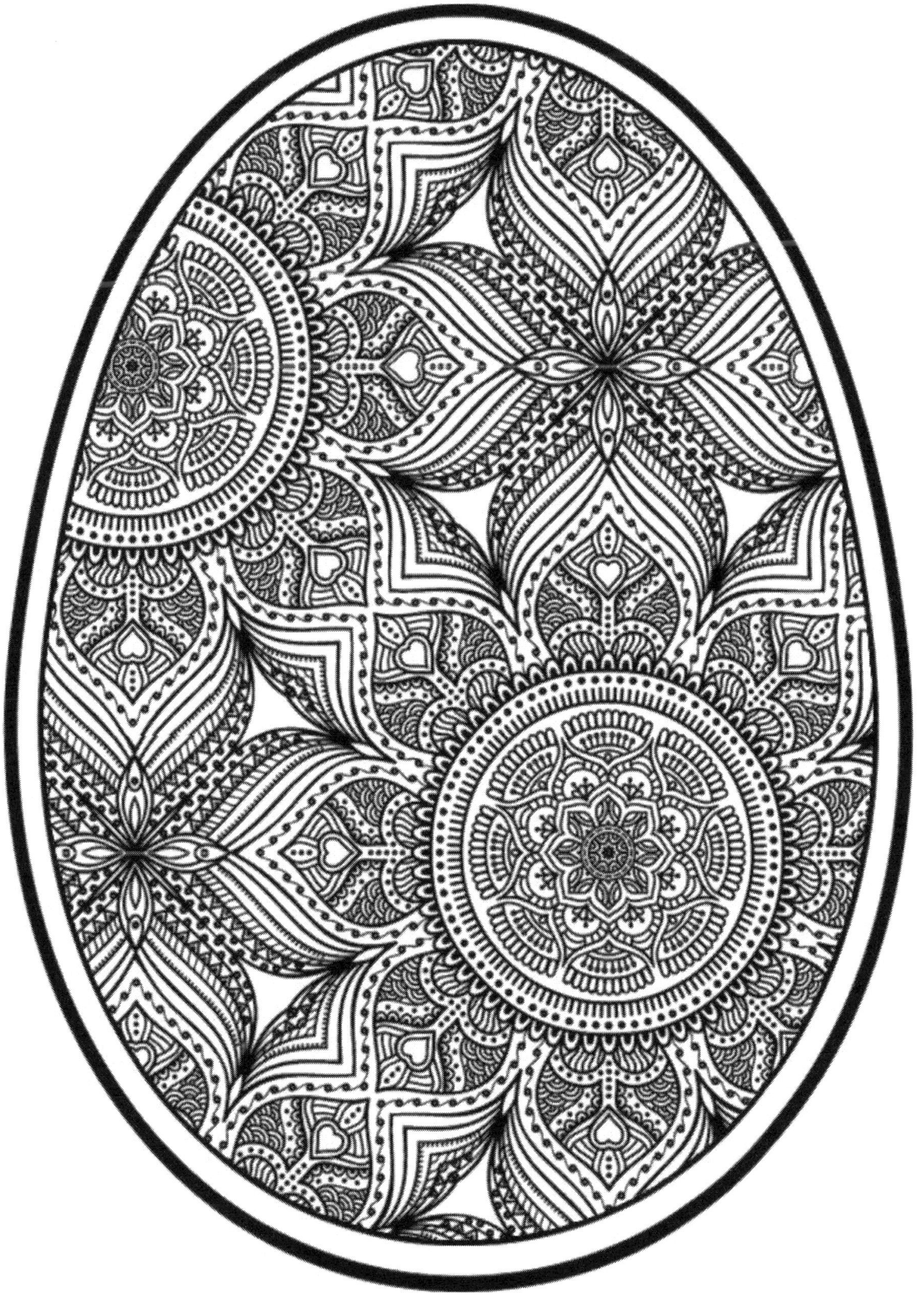

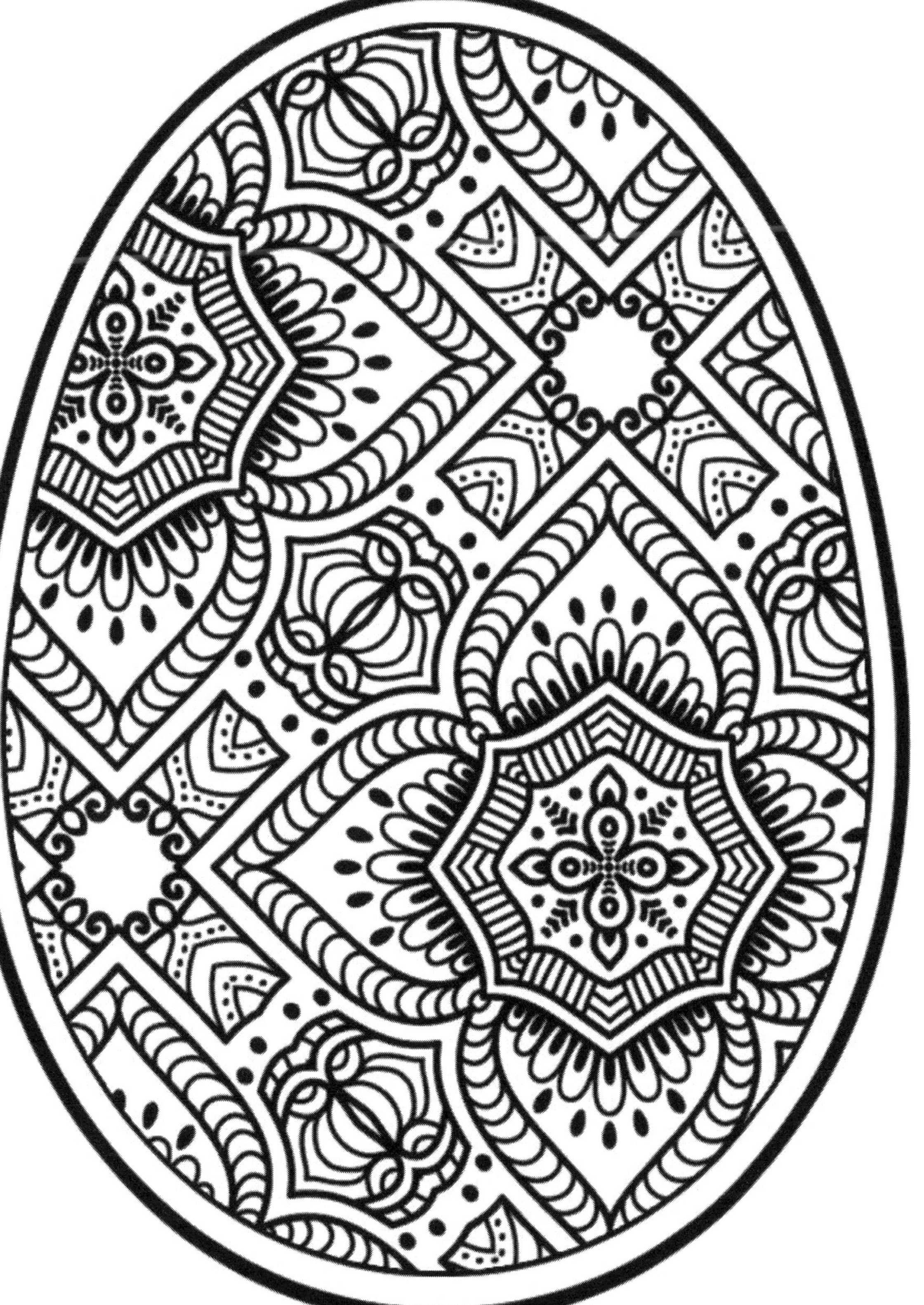

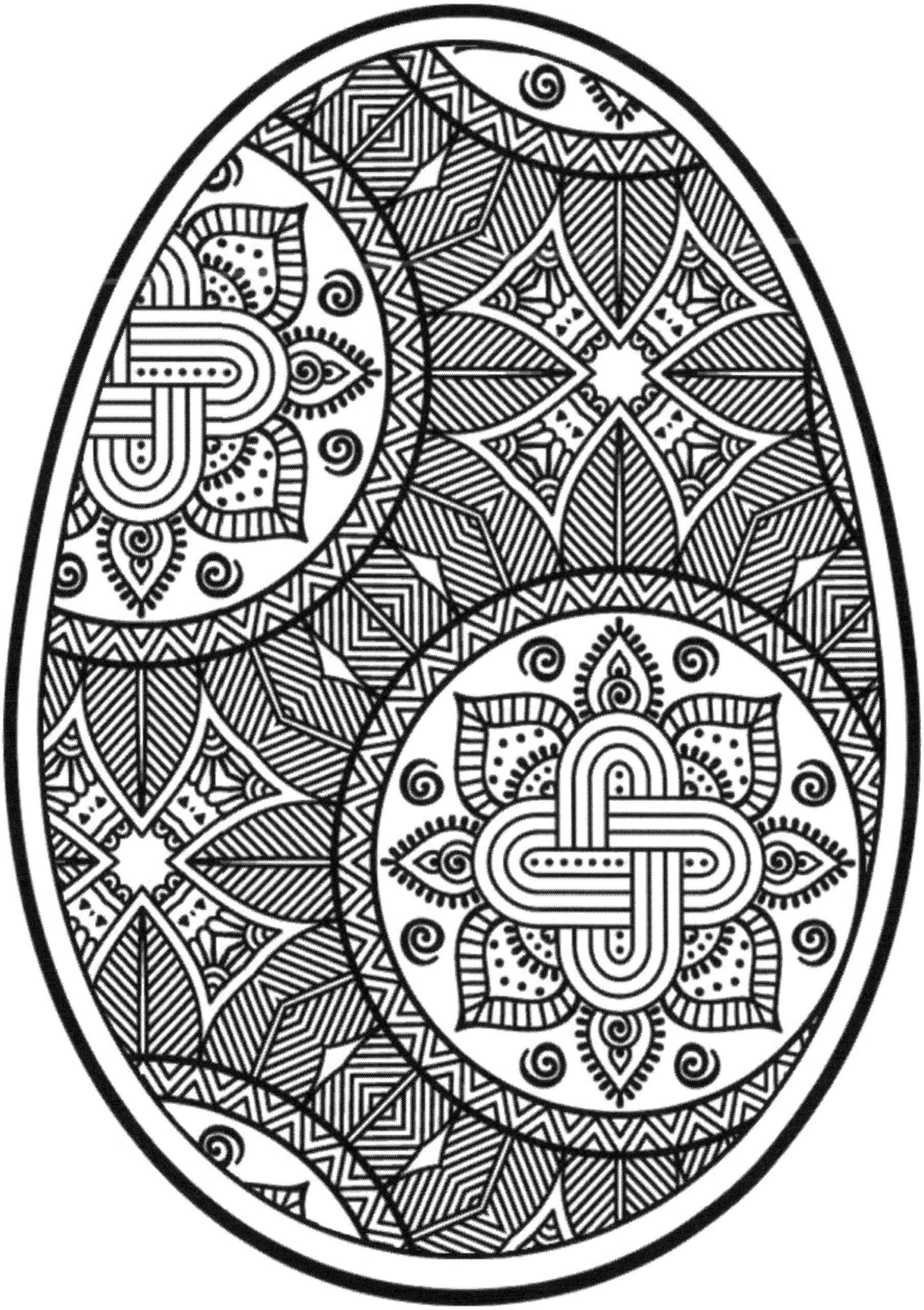

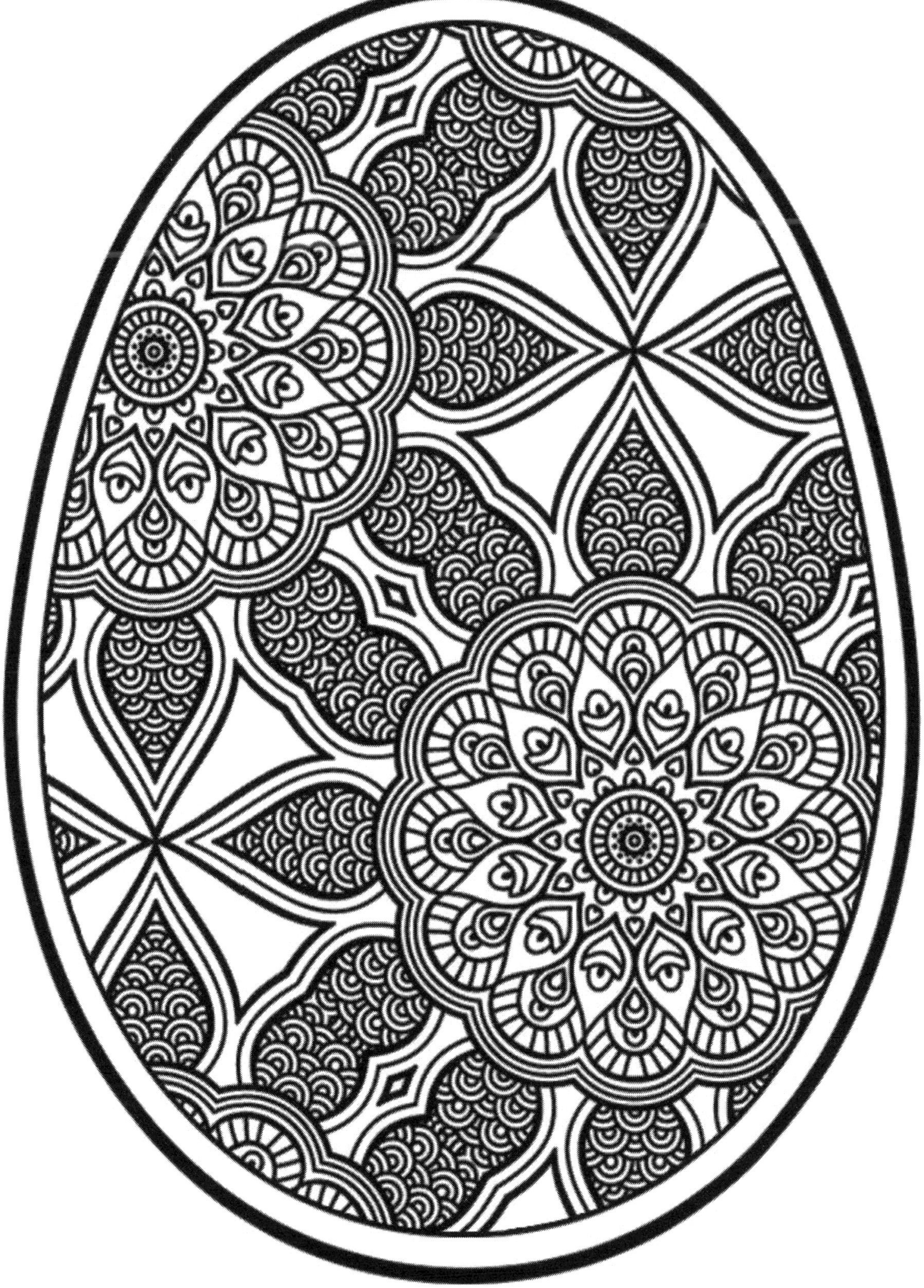

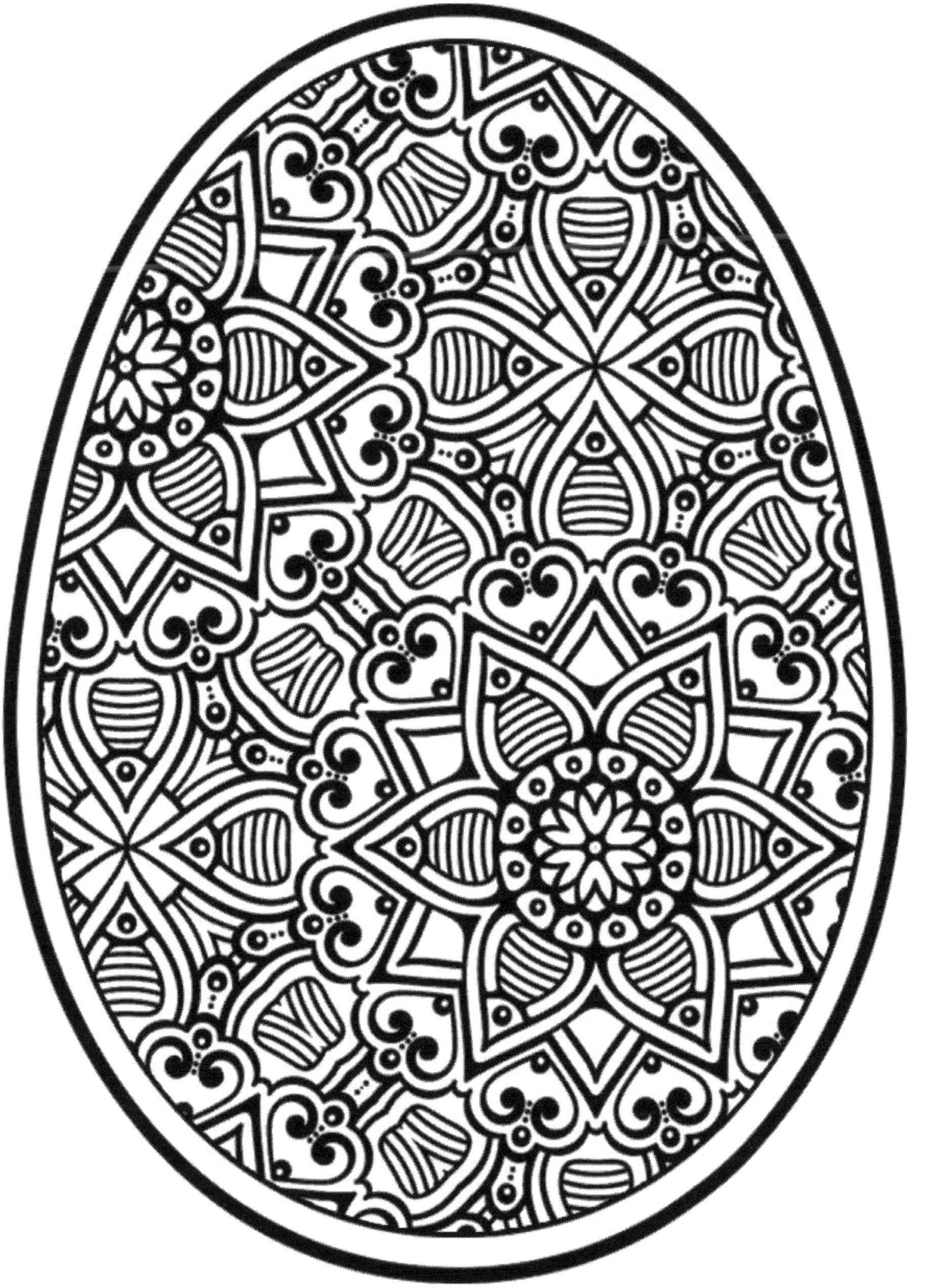

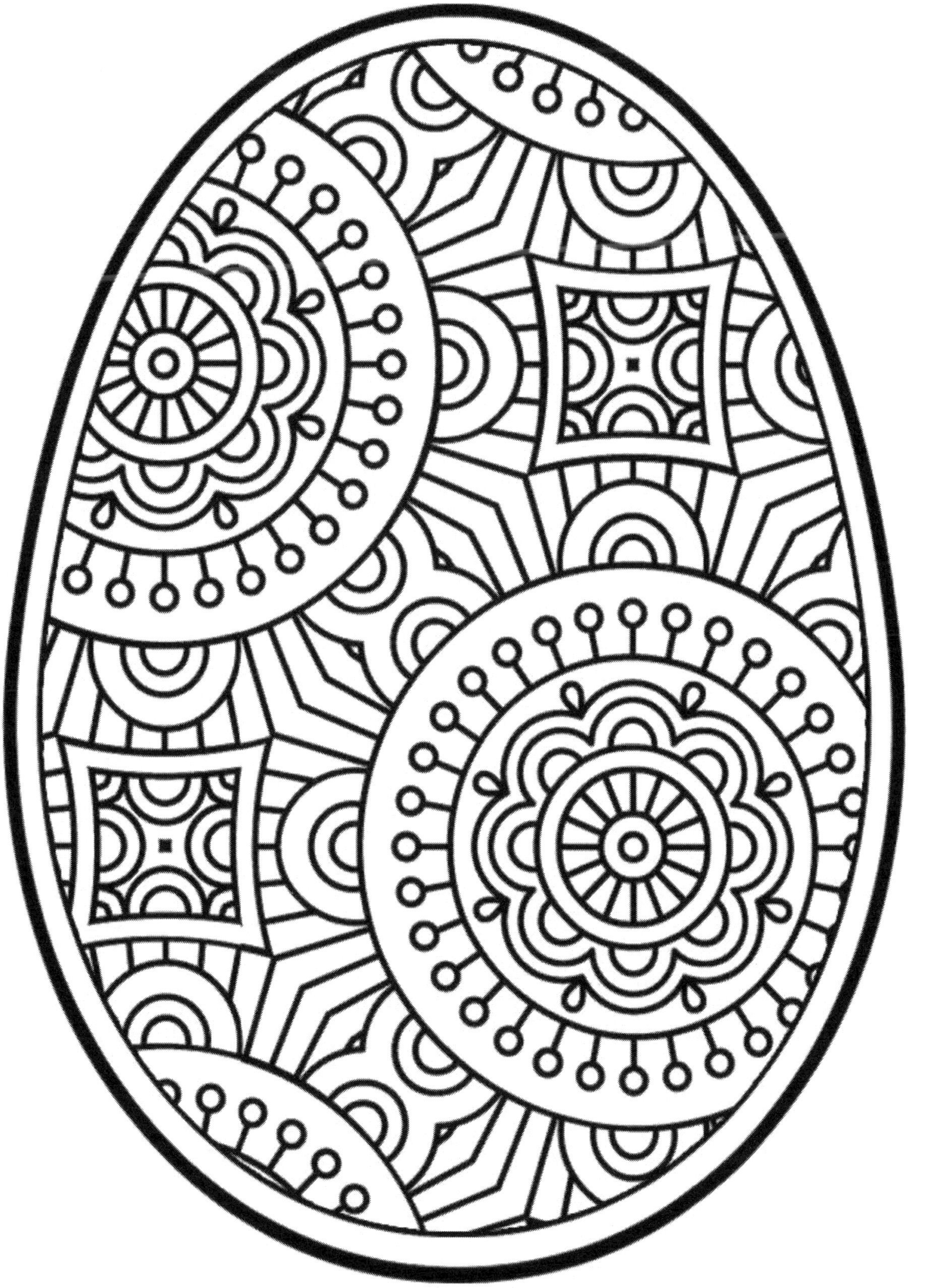

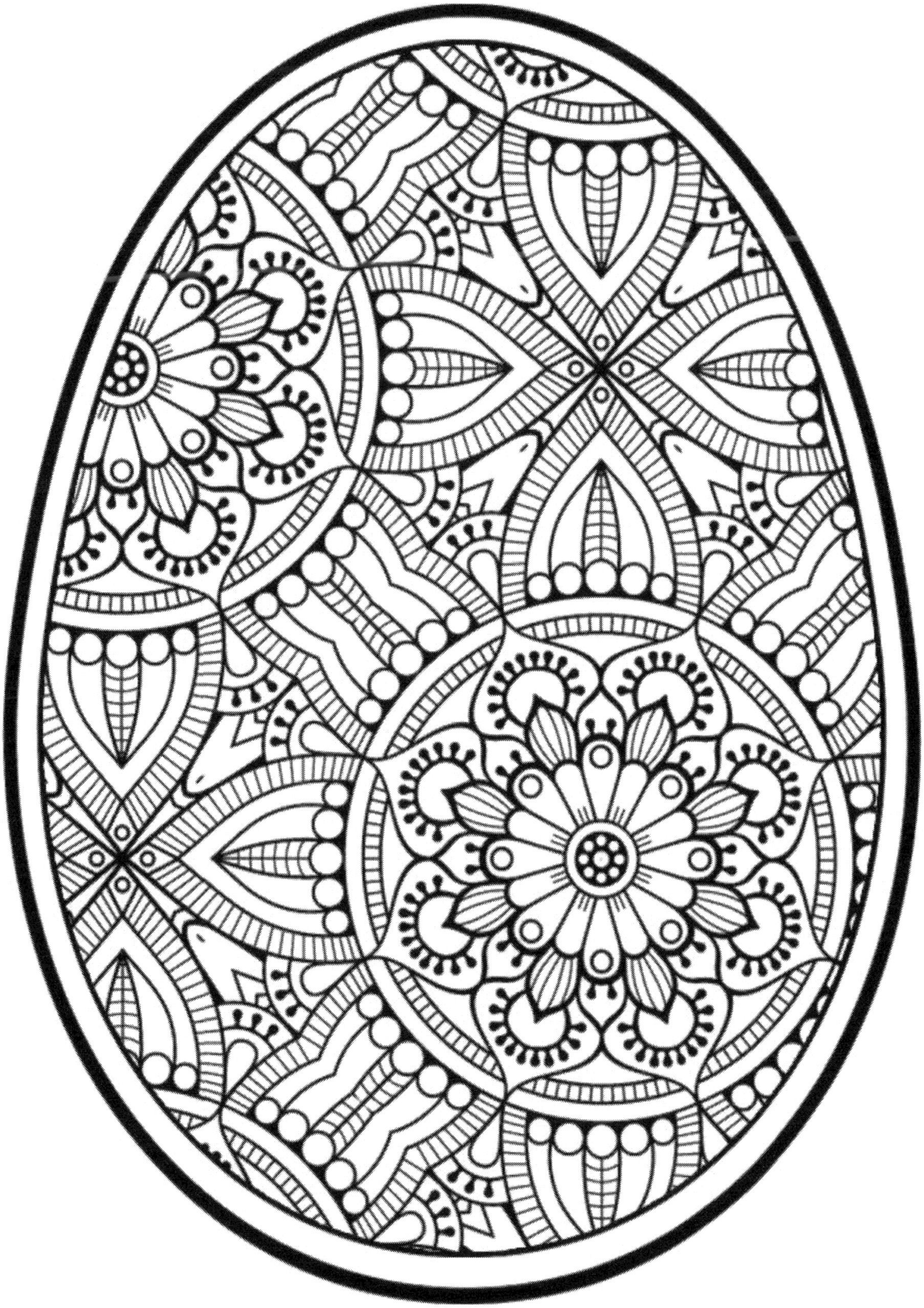

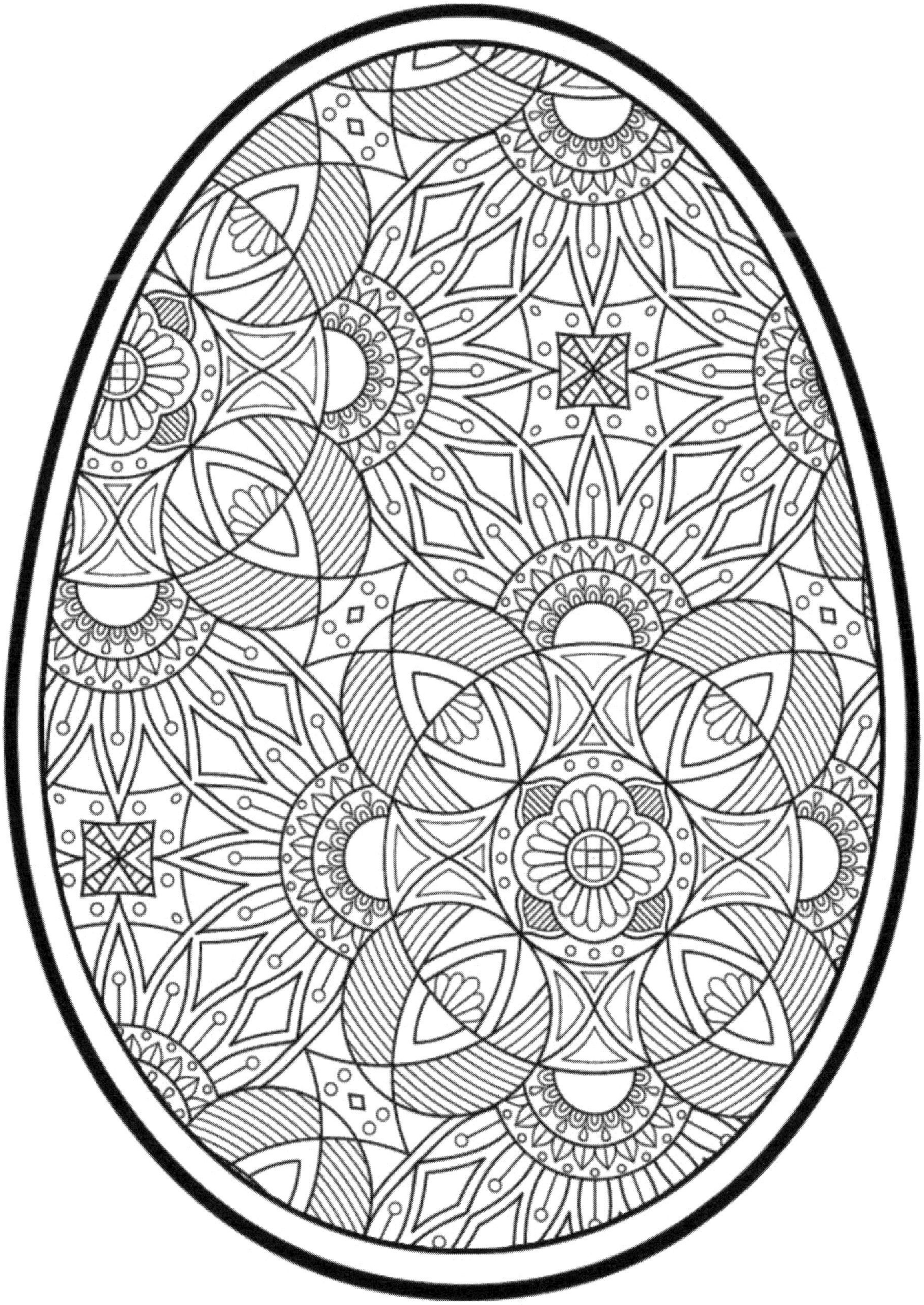

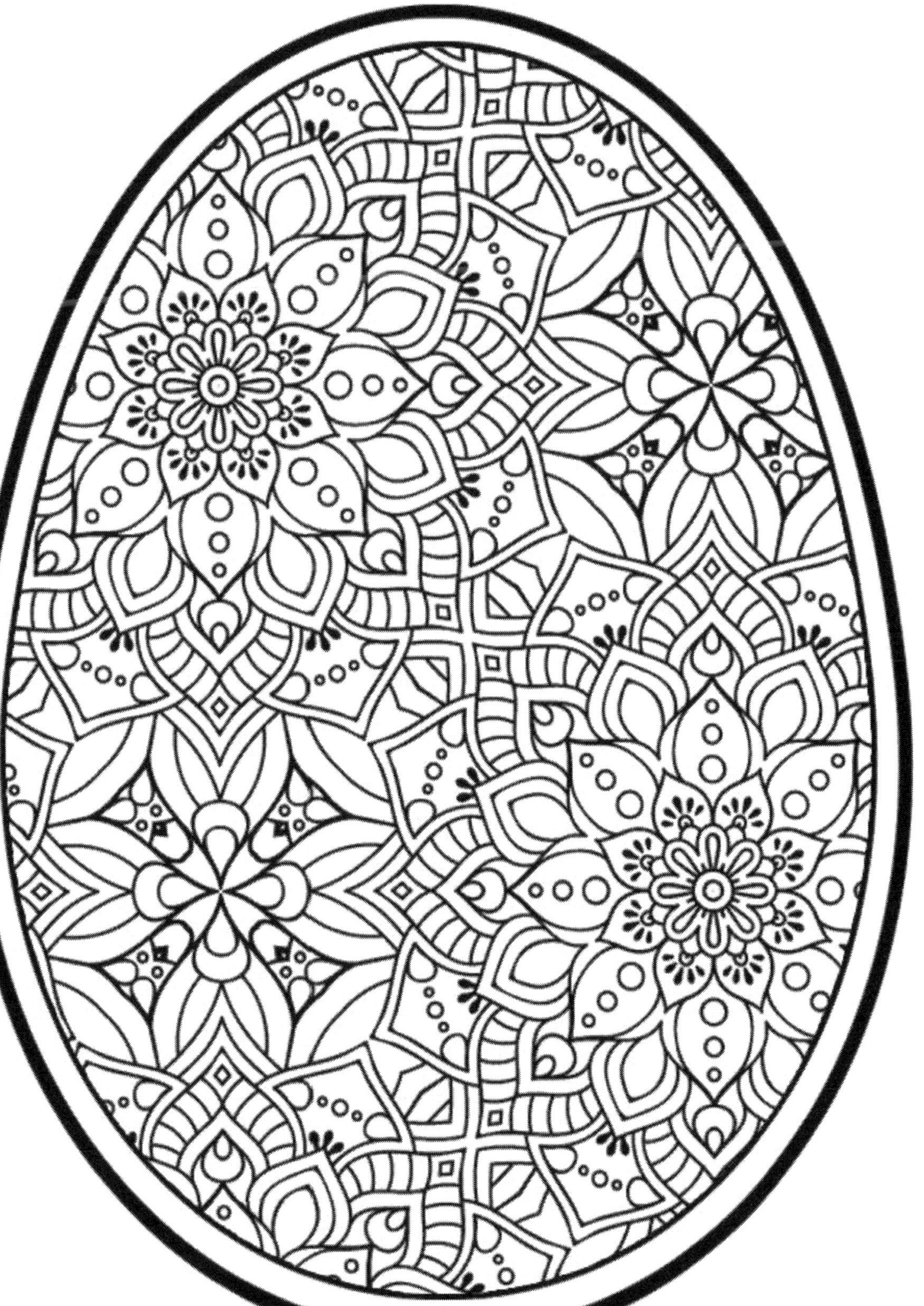

Made in the USA
Columbia, SC
28 February 2021

33673649R00059